# Swayed

## How to Communicate for Impact

## Christina Harbridge

NOTHING BUT THE TRUTH, LLC

SAN FRANCISCO

Published in 2016 by Nothing But The Truth, LLC

NothingButtheTruth.com

Nothing But The Truth name and logo are trademarks of Nothing But The Truth Publishing, LLC.

LIBRARY OF CONGRESS CATALOGING-IN-PUBLICATION DATA

Harbridge, Christina

Swayed:

How to Communicate for Impact

Mickey Nelson, Editor.

Library of Congress Control Number: 2016907662

ISBN: 978-0-9972962-4-2 (paperback)

ISBN: 978-0-9972962-3-5 (ebook)

Printed in the United States of America

2017

Cover design by ALL Publications, Portland, Oregon

Levels of Context image design by Melissa Mahoney at Indigo Creative

First Edition

# Praise for
## *Swayed: How to Communicate for Impact*

*Swayed* provides thought-provoking ideas and real world examples on the power of context. More importantly, the book offers a wealth of deliberate practices for how to implement in everyday life. This is not just a business book, it is essential reading for improving communication and increasing influence.

Simon Cowell, CEO, bareMinerals

I've been waiting for this book for years! I am so inspired by Christina's ability to inspire people to act and, more important, her ability to teach others how to do the same. Now we can all learn what she's mastered for years—how to sway people and inspire them to move forward.

Simon Sinek, Optimist and author of *Start with Why* and
*Leaders Eat Last*

*Swayed* is one of the most realistic and original books on influence you'll ever read. It doesn't just share one-off persuasion strategies. Instead, it helps you see and act compassionately, so you're seen as a trustworthy—and therefore influential—human being. A major contribution to the field. Thank you for writing it, Christina.

Mark Levy, Author of the O'Reilly Media course,
"Influencing People Honestly: Ethical Persuasion Strategies
for Leaders, Managers, and Entrepreneurs"

Christina has significantly changed the lives of five of the most important leaders in my life. Here, in a profoundly simple model, she's captured the essence of how she makes great people even more effective. I will be recommending this book to my closest friends. Bravo.

Mike Maddock, Founding Partner of Maddock Douglas, McGuffin Creative Group and Ringleader Ventures

Do everything this book says.

Amy Critchett, Founder, Art & Audience and Executive Producer, The Bay Lights

As someone who has worked very closely with Christina Harbridge over the years, I am thrilled that she has put her brilliant communication insights into an approachable, easy-to grasp, practical, and compelling book. *Swayed: How to Communicate for Impact* is a must-read for anyone seeking to effectively communicate and refine their presentation skills. The book provides concrete and real-life examples to follow and implement. Christina is one of the most brilliant communicators I have ever encountered and I highly recommend her approach which has enabled me to achieve my desired communication outcomes and take my organization to the next level.

Andrea Dew Steele, Founder, Emerge America

**This book is dedicated to:**

Sebastian: my reason for being. ILY MEP, Mom

&

Sonia: the person who quietly and tirelessly
makes it all possible.

# Contents

**Context:**
A simple concept that may solve 27%* of your
communication hiccups
*completely made-up statistic

# Introduction

Sit still for a moment and think about the most incredible inventions, events, or movements in history. You'll recognize that each began with people being able to influence others to join them. Influence is the beginning of nearly everything we create.

There is a moment in time when two or more people share the reality of a single thought and then sway the rest to movement toward a future outcome. When I think of the word *sway,* I feel such deliciousness in the idea that communication is a rhythmic practice—backward and forward or side-to-side like a rally or a dance. It is in this exchange that we have the power to set a new reality into motion.

Communication doesn't always feel delicious, though. It can be downright rough—in some cases nearly impossible to keep folks listening long enough to move a situation forward, let alone in the direction we prefer. To make matters worse, there are habits we all have around communication that can make the person swaying us feel like a direct assault or at least something to resist. There is better way! Here we will learn to identify natural human tendencies around communication, to use them to read situations, and to proceed in ways that will bring us closer to our desired outcomes.

This book is about a model—or a set of actions—that can change the way you listen and are heard and thus can improve the way you sway those around you. The Context Model, if used correctly and often, can solve many common communication challenges and repercussions of miscommunication. It is an exploration into how we can communicate in ways that increase our influence and move us closer to what we want.

### See if you can identify the challenges in the list below:

- Does it seem increasingly difficult to get and hold people's attention?
- Do you hear a lot of people in your company complain and yet the complaints do not seem to lead to change?
- Does your physiology become awkward or do you get stuck in your head when you're speaking publicly?
- Are communication problems causing misunderstandings? Do these miscommunications become time-consuming and disruptive?
- Is it often unclear what your boss/spouse really wants?
- Do some people make it impossible for you to really listen to them?
- Have you ever given feedback that created defensiveness in the recipient—or gotten defensive yourself, when someone else gave you feedback?
- Do you think some people talk endlessly although no one understands what they are trying to say?
- Wouldn't it be nice to solve these issues at the cause instead of treating the symptoms?
- Do you find that long, bulleted lists, like the one you are reading now, can cause you to lose track of what the original question was?

If you answered yes to any of these questions, you are noticing what I notice about communication. A book search on Amazon for the term *communication* retrieved more than 355,000 results because communication is as *tricky as it is crucial*.

**If you feel it is difficult to get people to listen, to understand and to act accordingly, then you are not alone.**

Miscommunication is a common challenge that is pervasive and often delays or disrupts outcomes we want. However, it is easier to solve than we make it.

**This book describes one model you can apply to any vertical in life (raising kids, love relationships, collaborating at work, public speaking, you name it).**

A model is a theory that is useless unless there are deliberate practices attached to it. Within this book you will have some of those practices to play with, and you must use them to make the model work for you. If used properly and regularly, the tools provided here may improve your understanding of those around you as well as enhance your ability to communicate effectively and influence others.

### Why just one model?

I have read a lot of books on communication that provide tons of ideas on how to improve a specific skill like conflict resolution, public speaking, or feedback. It is really hard to keep all those ideas in practice because the events that necessitate using them don't usually happen often enough to develop habits. Because we get good at what we do all the time, I picked just **one** model you can practice all the time. Then you will develop habits that can be applied to any communication situation.

Changing behavior can be hard. However, when you practice one model as a deliberate practice over and over, it becomes easy to behave in new ways—ways that can increase your ability to sway and influence. Think of this as sort of a slacker's guide to communication.

I've written this book with the belief that "how you do anything is how you do everything," as T. Harv Eker says, and that we get better when we practice something until it becomes a habit. I've provided you with both personal and professional examples throughout this book. When we practice influence in all areas of life, we form habits that show up in our toughest influence moments. Communication is not as easy as we would like, nor is it as hard as we make it. Through consistent experiment and practice, we can use influence to move a little closer to what we want.

At the end of each chapter, I give you simple, deliberate practices to accelerate your influence. As you read these practices, you may want to stop reading the book and simply focus on that practice for a few days before continuing.

### For those who want to *Sway* without reading the instruction manual

If you are someone who likes to jump ahead without following instructions, here is the Context Model, the solution to many influence challenges.

In this visual, you are seeing the different levels of context a person can communicate. People talk and listen at varying levels of context. The trick is choosing a level of context that fits the influence outcome we are trying to achieve.

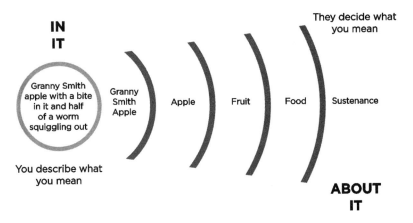

Let's apply CONTEXT to the challenges we mentioned in the previous list:

- Does it seem increasingly difficult to get and hold people's attention these days?
  - People often listen less if the conversation is vague, has too many buzzwords, or if there is too much preamble. Others may listen less if there is more detail. How does your listener listen?

    Action: Notice how your listener listens and match their level of context for greater influence.


- Do you hear a lot of people complain in your company, and yet the complaints do not seem to lead to change?
  - Telling a person to "collaborate" (a buzzword) doesn't always change behavior.

    Action: Notice if your requests include a SPECIFIC action the person can say yes or no to. If you are on the receiving end of a vague request or broad sweeping statement, make sure to ask for a specific example.

- Does your physiology get awkward, or do you get stuck in your head, when you're speaking publicly?
  - Getting out of your head and into the moment through detail and specificity can uptick your physiology in presentations. Storytelling does not have as much impact if it is too vague.

    Action: If you are opening a presentation with a story, start in the middle of the story with lots of action, color and example. People listen most to stories that have rich details.

- Are communication problems causing misunderstandings? Do these miscommunications become extremely time-consuming and disruptive?
  - Broad, sweeping statements at the "fruit level" often feel like personal attacks and can reduce influence.

    Action: Notice if you are using "labels" that cause people to be defensive or reactive. Use examples instead. Asking for an example can invest in a person's need to feel understood and help us improve a conflict situation.

- Is it often unclear what your boss/spouse really wants?
  - Are they asking us by using general language that we think we understand, but perhaps don't?

    Action: Listen for unclear descriptors and ask for examples.

- Do some people make it impossible for you to really listen to them?
  - Look closely at the model: are you only listening to people who communicate at your level of context?

    Action: Get curious about what level of context you listen in and practice communicating the way the person you are trying to influence listens.

- Have you ever given feedback that created defensiveness in the recipient—or gotten defensive yourself when someone else gave you feedback?
  - Is the problem that the feedback was not specific enough?

    Action: Remove the labels and superlatives from feedback and use examples to strike up a constructive conversation.

- Do you feel like some people talk endlessly, while no one understands what they are trying to say?
  - Are they talking in broad terms or specific terms? Knowing what kind of communication bugs you can positively affect your influence with people who do not communicate the way you do.

    Action: Notice if the person is talking ABOUT something (using a lot of generalities) and ask for an example. Notice if the person is giving TOO MUCH detail and ask them questions to move toward the relevant content.

- Wouldn't it be nice to solve these issues at the cause instead of treating the symptoms?
  - Influence is a practice in curiosity. This book provides practices to make it easier to influence when it can be difficult.

> Action: Practice noticing how people listen and how you talk. Use CONTEXT to drive curiosity.

For a more in-depth look at this model, please see Chapter Five.

# Section One

# A Reality Check on Being a Human Being

**I must begin with this reality check: *Humans are irrational and emotional.***

In this section I will first give some examples of the reality of miscommunication. We humans do not always behave in ways that get us closer to what we truly want, especially when it comes to communication. This section describes how poor communication interrupts us from getting the outcomes we truly want. An acknowledgment of how much we obstruct our desired outcomes due to poor communication drives commitment to better practices in the future.

To get the most out of this model of communication, see if you can find yourself in these common communication realities.

# Chapter One

# Behavior

**We do not always behave in ways that move us closer to what we want.**

Here is a pattern that occurs in my life. Does it sound familiar to you?

- There is an outcome I want.
- There are other people involved in achieving that outcome.
- Something happens and I get triggered (in other words, reactive) emotionally.
- I do or say something that moves me away from the outcome I want.

If this *doesn't* sound familiar, you may want to pinch yourself to make sure you're human because let's get real: Being irrational comes with the territory of being a person. Irrationality is part of what makes us beautiful, but it also complicates things by messing with our intentions and desired outcomes. To help you find yourself in what I'm saying, below are two examples, one personal and one professional.

## An example of a personal, triggered interaction

*Joe and Suzy are divorced. They have a daughter named Sophie who is nine. The desired outcome they share is raising her into a healthy woman.*

*One day Suzy is waiting at a slightly ajar door for Joe, who is late even though it is his one and only time a week to spend quality bonding time with their daughter. Suzy is not happy with Joe for a lot of reasons, the most immediate being his tardiness.*

*When Joe finally knocks, a little louder than Suzy prefers, on the door and Suzy lets him in, he immediately makes a comment about how messy Suzy's house is. Suzy stands up for herself and fires back a biting retort that, to her, makes the situation feel more fair. Their daughter stands there in the verbal crossfire. Joe and Suzy exchange more mean words, and then Joe abruptly leaves with his daughter, annoyed and irritated.*

What happens to the outcome Suzy wanted? Is Joe bonding with his daughter? Is he going to drive cautiously with Sophie in the car if he is upset?

How Suzy responded to Joe may have felt "fair" to her—yet it didn't get her what she wanted. Rationally, Suzy knows that the outcome she wants—her daughter to grow into a healthy woman—will be accelerated by a healthy relationship with her dad. Yet instead of creating an interaction that will help her achieve that outcome, she engaged in a dialogue that led to her daughter being driven away in a speeding car, seated next to an unfocused parent who is too angry at his ex-wife to connect with her.

Who's at fault in this example? Frankly, who cares? Suzy has moved far away from her desired outcome because her reaction in the moment trumped her long-term desired outcome.

**If we are using our *rational* mind, the outcome has to be more important than the moment.**

In a purely logical world, Suzy's and Joe's daughter Sophie is more important than making that moment more fair. It doesn't really matter who is right or wrong. Right or wrong shouldn't matter if we are being rational. However, even though exhibiting rational behavior moves us closer to outcomes we want, we fail to do it all the time. We get so focused on what *should* happen and on reacting to what we feel in the moment that we do not *act* in a way that moves us closer to our desired outcome. Can you think of a time you sabotaged yourself in this way? How could you have reacted differently?

**If we are more thoughtful or "at choice" in our actions, we are more likely to act toward what we want.**

To be more at choice in our behavior takes curiosity and practice. It may feel so simple and obvious as a theory. However, it is only with deliberate, repeated practice that we can influence results and get the outcomes we want.

As with the examples in this chapter, the outcome we want often requires the participation of another person. To influence the other person, saying exactly what we think in a given moment may not move us closer to the outcome we want. Often our communication in moments of reaction does the opposite of what we really want.

Please note that I am not advocating ignoring, numbing, or pretending. It's okay Suzy did what she did in the previous scenario—her reaction was valid and warranted. I am offering another way to look at the situation so Suzy could decide what is in *her* best interest. When I face situations like this, I try to selfishly focus on the outcome I want so I can move closer to it rather than allowing my irrational self to be distracted by a jab from another person. And actually, if Suzy had focused on her daughter becoming a healthy adult instead of reacting to old wounds with her spouse, her action could have been the opposite of selfish. Getting what we want isn't selfish, especially if we aren't hurting anyone in the process.

I promised a professional example as well. Why? You may not be able to find yourself in the personal example. Outcomes also get delayed at work as people communicate in ways that obstruct listening and understanding.

---

## Example of the founder of a company getting less of what she wants because of her behavior:

---

*Allison, the founder of a company, has hired smart people to be on her team—many of them experts in their verticals. Allison knows she has to let these people be the experts they are at their respective functions. She is a compassionate, patient and caring boss 95% of the time, but like all of us, sometimes she can be a bit brutal in her communication. It has been a tough week for Allison, her largest client is putting the next contract out for bid to get a lower price, she just had a rough meeting with her Board of Directors and the finance team made a costly mistake. She is stressed. In a meeting with her team she gets frustrated by their excuses, interrupts the explanation of the number of errors on the website, and screams, "If you can't fix this site, I need to find someone who can!"*

*The smart people Allison hired react to this broad, sweeping statement that she screamed emotionally. One person thinks, Go ahead, see if we can perform in these conditions. Another just shuts down entirely and doesn't say another word in the meeting. A third thinks about leaving the company for somewhere else he will be appreciated more. Allison leaves the meeting feeling like her team will not care more about the problem and fix it.*

The outcome Allison wants is to solve a business problem using the smart people on her team, and let's not judge her for being upset. If we simply look at this common scenario without emotion, what she needs to fix the business problem is information and a team rallying together to solve the problem. The way she communicated in the meeting caused her to not hear the explanation with details that may actually include her as part of the problem. Her behavior in the meeting moves her away from the outcome she wants. Hopefully, the team rallies and fixes the problem, but sadly, instead poor Alison will either lose good people or reduce their confidence and commitment to her company. Commitment matters when communicating as a leader. Alison didn't communicate in a way that created commitment.

Not very rational, is it? I have done this—acted in a way that didn't get me what I ultimately wanted. Have you? The thing is, Allison may rarely lead with an outburst like the above. The moment described may only happen once. Yet it is those moments when we make people feel small that can reduce our influence over time.

## There is no right way to influence.

As you read this book, notice if you become binary: use either/or thinking. Nothing in this book implies there is one **right** way or one **correct** way to influence. What I offer are other options that may help you move closer to the outcome you want. Although there is no **right** way to influence, there is always **another** way to influence. There is no **one** way to handle a conversation, conflict, or communication.

## Influence requires us to be willing to do something different from what our impulses drive us to do *in the moment.*

In order to use some sassy tool for communication, we must first go back to the concept of being "at choice" in our behavior. What this means is that our individual operating systems must be open and willing to choose the habit (and resulting action) that will move us closer to what we want.

When we can't influence, we can get annoyed, frustrated, and irrational. The irrational part may be hard for you to hear; I may lose you forever by accusing you of being irrational. It's not just you, however; I am irrational, too. In the following chapters, I'll give you some examples of how we often act irrationally when it comes to influence.

In order to influence, we must be less reactive and more activated. We will focus on one tool that you can practice in many ways, all the time, to help you increase influence, listening, and understanding in communication.

It is human to get annoyed rather than activated or "in choice," but we can change that.

## The key to influence is to study the other person and notice:

What makes a person listen? *Do more of that.*

What makes a person check out? *Do less of that.*

If we are focused on how a person listens rather than on being upset that the person isn't listening, we can build more influence.

---

### Example of a salesperson not talking in the way his prospective customer listens:

---

*Ken is trying to sell an accounting software to a local county hospital. On Ken's last few pitches, the COO of the hospital interrupted him, asking about capital expenditures. That interruption threw Ken off his game. He got very frustrated, showed it and said "If you could just be patient, I'd get there . . ."*

If Ken were rational, he'd **start** with capital expenditures, because that's clearly where the COO is most interested. If the COO is the decision maker, it only makes sense to formulate the pitch to speak to him directly. Even so, Ken shows his frustration, which creates an odd relationship with the very person who is going to decide whether to work with him or not. It would make rational sense for Ken to develop a presentation that is flexible enough to begin with the part the listener cares most about.

---

## Example of a mom changing her strategy to talk in the way her kids listen:

---

*Polly wishes her three sons, Lance, Sean and Steve, would listen to her. Every day she asks them to put their dirty laundry in the hamper and every day that request turns into a rant. She talks but they don't listen.*

*Polly notices how competitive her sons are, so she decides to attach a basketball hoop to the hamper. She puts blue painter tape with "2 points" and "3 points" on the bamboo floor. That night she hears the boys competing as they throw their smelly laundry through the hoop and into the hamper. Her mother-in-law Sue complains that Polly is not teaching the kids discipline and that she should instead punish the boys—by taking away their XBOX, for example—unless they clean up their stuff every night. Polly recognizes that is one way to influence her kids, but for now she likes the peace that comes with her fun, effective and quicker way. She runs downstairs with a silver whistle and acts like a basketball commentator as the boys toss their laundry from down the hall. There is laughter instead of stress. She got the outcome she wanted.*

In this example, Polly develops a workaround for the situation. What she does—turning a chore into something her sons enjoy and getting the outcome she wants—is a form of influence.

---

### Example of trying to convince someone who doesn't report to you to do something:

---

*Mike has tried to convince the IT department to set up the phone, computer, and badge for new employees' desks before they arrive for work. He has tried everything—begging, pleading, threatening—yet still, IT rarely has everything on the desk set up on time. One day on the way into work, Mike realizes, "Why do I have to start new employees at their desks first thing on their first morning? The IT department always has the desks set up by noon. Instead of knocking my head against a wall in frustration with the IT department, how about I create a new 'first day' for new employees that will keep them away from their desks until noon when the desk is ready?" Instead of spending his influence dollars investing in a 9 a.m. start time, Mike changes his new-employee routine.*

In this example, Mike develops a specific workaround for the situation. What he does—getting specific about solutions rather than suffering and complaining—is also a form of influence.

## The key to influence is to practice an outcome-focused way of thinking.

The key to influence is figuring out what makes an individual listen and what makes that person check out, and then tailoring your message and delivery appropriately. Influence is also about trying to do things to get to the outcome you want.

Too often we get so focused on our own preferences that we

forget about our desired outcome. If people aren't listening, you can't influence them. If they do not listen when you talk, you must change how you talk in order to influence them. THAT is rational, and not always easy to do.

---

## Example of trying to influence a boss by talking the way she listens:

---

*Carol is the CEO of a boutique branding company. She sits in production meetings on her handheld most of the time unless someone tells a story about a customer.*

*Pete is the CFO of a large manufacturing company. He checks out if anyone is talking about innovation or uses the buzzword* disruption. *He checks IN when anyone says* consistency, systems *or* process.

*Joe has to present an idea to Carol and Pete. When he is preparing his three-minute presentation, he makes sure he has a 45-second customer story, and he talks about refining the process in sales. He avoids pushing his idea as a new innovation and instead focuses on how his idea adjusts the process to better fit customers' needs.*

Joe is able to keep both parties listening a little bit longer by communicating in the language they hear best and not triggering them to disengage by saying words he knows makes them check out.

## The question regarding influence isn't "What am I doing?" It is more "How is it working?"

The question to be asking yourself throughout your day is, Am I communicating in a way that focuses the conversation toward the outcome desired? or, Is the action I am taking getting me more of what I want?

So often we communicate by default rather than by design. We let outcomes slip away because we aren't actually thinking about what we really want.

---

## A personal example shows how the influencer changed outcomes by changing self:

---

The following true story is a perfect example of how we often communicate by default rather than by design. I have changed the names and a few details so folks keep their privacy.

*Mary is the founder of a construction company and she works constantly. She leaves the house at 7 a.m. and doesn't return until 7 p.m. Her partner, Pat, works at home with their three boys who are under the age of seven. Mary complains that Pat gives her way too much detail. Every night when Mary asks, "How was your day?" Pat gives her specifics about things she doesn't care about. She rolls her eyes, tunes out, and even walks away from Pat to avoid the conversation.*

*Pat doesn't feel listened to or cared for, and Mary doesn't feel interested. They both suffer. When Mary complained to her business coach about this, she was fairly upset. "Pat just gives me too much information! Blah, blah, blah!" The more she talked about it, the more frustrated she became. Years of frustration came spewing out onto the table. When she paused for a moment, her coach reached across the table and said, "Mary, you need to learn to ask better questions." For a brief moment, Mary thought about slapping her. Her coach gently added, "What is it you want to know about, Mary? I can help you come up with ways to hear more of what you want with your questions."*

*Mary got a little teary and said sadly, "I see my sons only for an hour or so a day. I am missing so much . . . I want to know about them and what I am missing I'd love to hear stories about the boys that do not include the words 'you need to talk to your son'." So, Mary and her coach came up with fifteen questions she could ask when she walked in the door. Questions like, "What did the kids do today that shows their individual character?" or "Tell me about the moments today you laughed out loud?" or "What did I miss today with the kids?" or "Any moments today that the kids tested your patience?" or "What do you want me to make for dinner while you go put your feet up?" Okay, that last question doesn't have anything to do with the kids, yet it may give Mary a happier marriage (wink).*

*After Mary used these new questions, she left her coach a voicemail about how the dynamics at home changed miraculously overnight. After Mary had told Pat the story, he bought a Flip camera so every day he and the boys could make short videos for their mom and show them to her when she walked in the door.*

A beautiful family ritual emerged all because Mary decided to stop the cycle of suffering by changing her own behavior. By asking for what she really wanted, she got what she really wanted.

## An example of an employee who wants a promotion:

*Theo wants a promotion. He has been passed over twice due to his "lack of experience." He is angry and begins to act passive-aggressively toward his boss. In 1:1 meetings Theo is either withdrawn or visually defiant. The relationship gets very uncomfortable. At his next review, Theo is dinged for his attitude. At the next promotion round, he isn't even considered.*

Theo is acting irrationally—in contradiction to his ultimate goal of getting the promotion. His company may be wrong in its promotion policies and he may be justified in being upset, yet his actions are harming his outcome. What should he do? Get closer to the decision makers and figure out what specifically he must do to prove he deserves the promotion (or accept that the promotion may never happen and make the choice to leave). Theo's boss may be the problem for him and his promotion, yet when he acts in ways that reduce influence with his boss he will get less of what he wants— whether he is justified in being upset or not.

## Our reaction to stimulus doesn't always rationally lead us where we want to go.

At this point, you may be wondering why humans communicate with a focus on effort rather than on the outcome they'd like.

Plainly said, in most situations, people would rather be right than be heard. I think this is a biological impulse. I am not a doctor—nor do I play one on TV—so I can't prove what

I'm writing in a lab or with some study. However, I do believe humans have a biological imperative to be right because I'm always seeing people act in a way that causes them to lose their long-term outcomes because they're so determined to be right.

---

## Here is an example in a marriage of two people forgetting the real outcome they want:

*Tim wants to have a beautiful dinner with his wife. She arrives home without the Chardonnay he asked her to pick up and he snaps at her for "always letting him down." Words are exchanged and they end up in a huge fight. The entire evening is shot because of Tim's impulse in the moment to verbally cut off his wife's head. What he really wanted to happen—a beautiful dinner—doesn't happen.*

What if, instead of focusing on the wine, Tim focuses on the outcome he wants? Sure, he can be frustrated about the forgotten wine, yet he can make a decision to let it go, send her out to get some, go next door and borrow some, open the bottle they have been hoarding for ten years, use a delivery service, make fancy drinks instead, or have an alcohol-free night. All these options are there to **still deliver** the evening Tim wants.

---

## An example of trying to land a deadline at work and missing an opportunity to influence:

*Jan needs her team members to commit to a project deadline, yet instead of seeking their commitment, she merely gets their compliance. She tells them what to do and how to do it rather than enrolling them in the end result. "The three of you hire the same vendors we used last quarter, offer them a bonus for hitting deadlines and authorize overtime for engineering at 11%." When her team tries to push back and ask questions, "The Hampshire Company didn't—" she cuts them off because she is pressed for time and believes she is communicating clearly. "Jan, we will draft a CNC—" Jan interrupts, "This is not a standard roll out, skip that." Jan can see that the team is unclear and disengaged, yet she leaves the meeting anyway. She doesn't get what she wants because she is in a hurry and not thinking about possible repercussions—and the team has not bought in.*

Instead, what if Jan stopped for a second and asked, "Hey, let's quickly align on what we have agreed to and sketch out a plan." Just one question may let her team tell her they aren't aligned. It is more rational to know **now** rather than later if her team is clear on how to achieve the new deadline. In the scenario above, the team had information that could have changed the trajectory of the project and sadly Jan didn't get the information as soon as she could have. (She will find out later and it will cost delays in the project.)

## In an argument, we often talk in such a way that causes the other person not to listen.

This doesn't make good sense, yet it is just what we do. We have a right to do it, right? Well, unfortunately this kind of thinking leads us to lose track of what we really want: *under-standing*. We're so busy feeling justified in being mad, we sacrifice our end goal. Our need to be right trumps our desire to be understood.

---

**For example, let's go back to Susie (who forgot the wine) and her husband, and see it escalate:**

---

*Tim shrieks at his wife, "YOU ALWAYS DO THIS!" She has forgotten the wine a couple of times in the course of their relationship, although not every time. She goes inside her head, thinking of all the times she hasn't forgotten, and she stops talking. He demands she talk to him, and she shuts down even further. She leaves the room. Their nice dinner is destroyed—and it's because of Tim's need to be right.*

We can all understand why Tim did what he did—and still it doesn't make sense when you think about what Tim really wanted. In that moment Tim was listening in response mode, ready to say something rather than trying to feel what she was feeling. His sway felt much more like a shove! Why is this?

**People listen to respond rather than to understand.**

I am not sure who originally coined that phrase. I have tried to find the author so I could buy her a year's supply of donuts, because this sentence completely changed the way I listen. When we listen to understand, we are filling a basic need. Humans have a basic need to feel understood, yet we often talk and listen in ways that violate that need.

We trigger people into responding and then blame them for responding in their own ways instead of the way we want them to. We often interrupt when they are trying to make themselves understood, and then we get mad at them for being angry with us. This book gives you a tool to listen to *understand*, therefore increasing influence.

A Deliberate Practice

Practice staying focused on the *outcome* you want and getting curious about how to use what is happening to move closer to that outcome. Curiosity can be a cure for miscommunication.

The ability to choose behavior that moves us closer to the outcome we want is a practice that begins with the realization that our reactive ways can get us less of what we really want. When we become focused on outcomes and become more curious about how we are being heard and what the other person is communicating, we are more likely to be able to act "in choice."

*What is the outcome I want and how do I use what is happening to move closer to that outcome?*

# Chapter Two

# Rainbows and Unicorns
# Will Not Appear

**Influence is practice, not promises.**

I get very turned off by products that make promises I know they can't deliver, so let's start by setting realistic expectations about communication and influence.

Do not expect rainbows and unicorns to suddenly appear around you. Influence is iterative: The results will be inconsistent because every human is different. We listen how we listen in a given moment. We change as people and what works one minute may not work the next. Stay flexible. You will need to *practice* playing with all of this.

**You must take absolute responsibility for increasing influence if you want to get anywhere.**

If they aren't listening, it's your problem, not theirs. That may sound harsh, but it's the cold, stark reality of influence. It's up to you to do what it takes to get their attention. If you don't, then they won't listen, and if they don't listen, then you won't get what you want. They'll go on their merry way and you'll be left flapping in the wind, unsatisfied.

## An example of an organization with a
## listening problem that will mess with outcomes:

*An engineer knows his gaming company must immediately focus on shifting its platform to a handheld. Even though he presents the idea thoughtfully, the executive team doesn't listen. He gets angry and gives up.* If they are too stupid to see the reality they are facing, *he thinks,* then that's their problem. *In his irrational state, he fails to realize that he presented the information in such a way that they couldn't hear it. He presented from an engineering perspective rather than a sales/user perspective. He had so many slides to prove the what and how of the change, he forgot to focus the executives on the why in terms of revenue gain. He doesn't see that, he blames them for not listening and becomes despondent. He forgets that his stock options are his only plan for retirement, and if the company fails, it will destroy that plan. Over the next few months, a competitor shifts its platform, and 60% of his company's customers jump ship.*

The engineer has a really good "I told you so" story—which he tells while standing in the unemployment line. Because what the engineer wanted to happen didn't happen. The fact that the executives did not listen to him was ultimately as much his problem as it was theirs. Ouch. Please note, the executives SHOULD freaking listen and if you are one, notice if you are discounting people who do not translate into your language. Good communication can happen if one of the parties is focused on influence and understanding outside of their preference. The job of a leader is to confront reality sooner and improve upon it. They didn't listen and it hurt their career. Don't let either of the people in this story be you.

It is your problem if those you are influencing aren't listening to you, because what you want to have happen, won't happen. That is a problem. You must figure out how to get them to listen if they are part of the outcome you are trying to achieve. If you live the belief that it is their fault for not listening, you likely will not change how you try to influence them. Then, your outcome won't happen.

**Any time miscommunication happens, it is your own fault.**

I get a lot of pushback over that sentence. Here's why it is true and hard: If the miscommunication is your fault, you have the power to change something to make it better. It isn't that they aren't listening to you; it is that you haven't figured out how to get them to listen. This orientation will help you stay activated, motivating you to study the other parties involved and to come up with another way to influence them.

In the interest of full disclosure, please note there are times when I give up and leave people if I can't influence them. The principle of diminishing returns is real, and that is okay, too.

### Example of influence in a diminishing-returns situation:

*Tomika is head of sales in a software company that's going public. She has invested years of service to the organization. The new CEO is making choices that will hurt the customer. She has tried every way she knows how to influence the CEO and others to make better decisions. She realizes she must make a choice because what she is doing isn't working. She can leave, she can keep trying to influence, or she can simply focus on her role and her deliverables. She decides leaving isn't in her best interest because her stock will create quite a nest egg. She decides to focus the next 90 days on the deliverables that are in alignment with her values. It isn't that she has given up. She is just investing her energy where she has control. She ends up resigning nine months later when it is more financially sound for her. In those nine months she did well for the company and for herself.*

Often in situations like this, humans get binary (seeing things as **either/or** or **black/white**) and leave, to the peril of their own finances. There is value and power in leaving, too. Tomika's story can be told many ways—for example, the saddest version would be people sabotaging their own careers because they can't get someone else to listen. The point is this: We all have to decide how much we are willing to invest in influence, because it can be exhausting.

## Miscommunication is more in our control than we think it is. And it is hard.

We can't change another person. We can't get that French dude to understand English just by raising the volume of our voice. We will not change CEOs' minds by trying to force them to do something or hear something they do not want to do or hear. And we can't make an audience listen if it's not interested in what we have to say or how we say it.

Yet, we have more control than we think we do. We can focus on tailoring our messages to what is most interesting for the other person and steering a conversation in the direction we want it to go. Sometimes this means investing in influence by letting others drive the conversation.

*Courage is what it takes to stand up and speak;*
*courage is also what it takes to sit down and listen.*
—*Winston Churchill*

Instead of trying to change other people—an irrational act—we need to think about changing what *we* are doing in order to get better results. If we do this with curiosity and openness, we are more likely to influence. If we do this as a manipulator who only cares about what is in our own head, we will likely lose influence because what is happening in our head will show up in our behavior. Most of us just aren't good at being fake in the long term. We call this natural inclination our "operating system." It is our go-to source of reactions when we aren't being thoughtful about our reactions or our desired outcomes.

## Your operating system dictates whether you use this tool to accelerate understanding or use it as a weapon.

Like it or not, your operating system is driving a lot of your behavior. It is your go-to source of reactions when you don't think about what reaction you *really* want or how to get to your desired outcome. If you are physiologically triggered, you may behave in ways that move you away from what you want. Here is how to use context when your operating system takes you on autopilot.

## An example of knowledge not translating into new behavior in communication:

*Susie goes to a speech coach and is told not to put her hands in front of her like a fig leaf, but to have her hands at her sides unless describing an object. When she steps in front of a hostile room, her physiology shifts and she does the fig leaf gesture automatically.*

Knowing what she should do with her hands doesn't manifest the behavior Susie wants.

The more Susie thinks about what to do with her hands, the more likely she will experience the kind of physiological discomfort that causes people to put their hands in front of their bodies. This model can help with the *physiology* that is causing the fig leaf gesture.

**Physiology is driving much of our influence behavior.**

The Merriam-Webster dictionary defines physiology as "the organic processes and phenomena of an organism or any of its parts or of a particular bodily process." It took me a few seconds to understand that explanation, so I'll give you an easier one: how the stuff in our body that we cannot always consciously control (breathing, blood pressure, sweating, blood flow, larynx, etc.) functions. I believe at least 50% of communication is based on our physiology in the moment. Any work we do around influence focuses on what makes a person "physically" able to be more comfortable with discomfort. To be a great influencer, we must become better at "being okay with not being okay." If something or someone makes us uncomfortable, irritated, or upset, how do we remain in control of our communication?

The tools in this book will help with some of your physiology, but if you aren't focused on the outcome, they will not be as effective. To truly influence, we must be a bit more deliberate in what we say or how we listen and react.

There is no single perfect solution for all situations; good communication requires **constant, curious, deliberate practice.**

Warning: Others using this way of communicating may try to use it as a weapon when they are feeling triggered. Expect those moments and get curious anyway. This model isn't a trick or an opening for deception. It is a *tool*—a new lens through which to view communication.

## A Deliberate Practice

A deliberate practice of being curious and flexible can increase your influence in an interaction. Making small changes in what you are doing without expecting miracles can keep you improving this skill. Here are some examples:

Don't be stuck in a rigid idea of how things should or must go.

Be a student. Allow for variances in outcomes and learn from them. Use what you discover to influence more effectively next time.

Stay open. Remember to ask yourself in moments of influence if you are open or closed. We cannot have influence if we are closed.

### *Am I open or closed?*

# Chapter Three

# Talk the Way They Listen

**We often reduce the outcome we want by the way we listen and/or talk.**

People often communicate in their own preferences rather than translating their message into the way others prefer to listen.

**Communicate by design rather than by default.**

We often spend a lot of time incorrectly designing our communication for *ourselves*. This leaves the way another person is influenced to happen by default.

There is a way to focus on how our physiology can (comfortably) translate into another person's way of listening. In other words, we recommend designing the conversation with the end user in mind rather than for you, the speaker.

Creating deliberate practices can help you apply the model in ways that will effectively move you closer to the outcomes you want. Be mindful that our behavior as humans varies hourly, so sometimes this model increases listening and other times you will need different tactics.

**A silly example of a preference:**
Fonts. *Fonts.* **Fonts.**

People's reactions to fonts can dictate how many sentences they read beyond a font style. If you have a preference for a font, you want your preferences satisfied. If a text uses a font that is not your preference, you may label the text a certain way. If you are someone with a profound preference for sans serif fonts, you may already have started a dialogue in your head without thinking too much about it.

This seemingly insignificant and silly font example could be *really important* in terms of engagement. With influence, we have preferences that drive our listening and attitudes toward what we are hearing. We all have our own setup preferences.

Good luck with *that.*

## Influence can be tricky because humans are so focused on themselves.

In order to listen we must be able to find ourselves in what *others* are saying. When we think about how many factors are involved when we're trying to get people to listen to and understand us, it becomes clear that doing this is not as easy as we might like it to be.

## Why is influencing people so freaking hard?

People listen in their own style and preference, not in yours.

Your liking the font I'm using here could make you a tiny bit more engaged in this writing. Your attention upticks a little when a preference you have is satisfied, and that makes you more likely to listen or read on. If this font is not your favorite, however, I've already lost part of your attention regardless of whether you agree with what I'm saying.

Our preferences show up in so much of our lives, especially in how we listen. We tend to hang out with people who are like us. We also tend to hang out with people who agree with us on things we care about. This is why silos form in companies, people get into cliques, and strangers bond so fiercely over sports. Next time you are out with your best friend, notice how many of your preferences are satisfied. Though not always, people generally hang out with folks who think the way they do. This innate preference causes us to **talk the way *we* listen rather than how *others* listen.**

That is fine for much of our day-to-day communication, but when it comes to the moment when you do need to influence people, it is imperative to consider not only your desired outcome but also who you are communicating with. The road to a desired outcome, therefore, is in how you listen.

Why this is hard: We like talking the way we talk. We have accepted (and may even like) the suffering we experience when we fail to adapt to others' listening preferences.

The more we think about ourselves and our preferences and wish people would listen differently than the way they do, the further away we are moving from the outcome we want. Communicating more rationally means figuring out how to translate our language into theirs (without being fake, gross, or pandering).

## Our preferences drive our listening behaviors.

People listen more to people and things they like. The model we use here doesn't dig into all specific preferences and how to translate, yet it does give you tools to get curious about how others listen. I mention this caveat here because I do not want you to think this book holds *every* key to influence. It holds one piece that, when practiced for a few weeks, can increase influence as long as you are also curious about the other person's preferences.

**Influencing others to listen isn't about increasing volume; it is more about translating into preferences.**

If someone doesn't understand what we're saying, many of us have a tendency to get louder and slower. It doesn't seem to work, yet we do it anyway.

---

## Here is an example you may have witnessed while on vacation:

---

*Susie, an American, is in France, and she is trying to order a dairy-free meal. The server Francois does not understand her, so Susie speaks more loudly and slowly and keeps saying the exact same words over and over. Instead of looking up "milk" or "dairy" on her phone (or even drawing a picture of a cow and drawing a line through it while holding her stomach), the word* dairy *becomes "DAAAARE-EEEE"—not a particularly rational move. What makes Susie's approach even more illogical is the fact that she knew she had a dairy allergy prior to walking into the Fromage Café—she could have looked up the word in advance so she could have this conversation in the language of the server. She didn't, and now she is frustrated and doing things that aren't going to move her any closer to the outcome she wants:*

*a healthy, enjoyable and dairy-free meal. (Note: Fromage means Cheese in French.)*

This scenario is a bit cartoonish, but it's one that happens way too often: Instead of getting individuals to listen by speaking in *their* language, we stay stuck in our own language and expect them to do the work to translate.

---

## An example of influencing someone into a preference at work:

---

*Otis reports to Tomas in the Data Science department. Tomas is highly organized and a very process-oriented person. Otis is not. Part of Otis's genius is his ability to perform in chaos. Prior to their meetings together, Otis spends a bit of energy creating an agenda for Tomas. This isn't Otis's preference, yet he has found that his meetings with Tomas go better with an agenda. Otis is influencing in the way Tomas listens rather than in the way Otis thinks. Otis doesn't like agendas, yet he knows if he uses them, the meetings have clearer communication.*

The goal of most communication moments is to increase understanding, yet often:

- We use our language instead of theirs.
- We repeat the same thing again and again, expecting them to suddenly understand.
- We give up instead of translating what we are trying to say into how they listen.
- We make the issue a flaw in the other person rather than

acknowledging that the problem is in part our failure to translate our language into something the other person can understand.

Spend some time trying to catch yourself repeating instead of adjusting your communication.

---

## An example of an attempt to influence someone at work who has different preferences:

---

*The head of engineering, Dan, needs the CEO, Carol, to make a decision about something. Carol doesn't like to listen to details and Dan knows this, yet he still goes into the meeting with 73 slides full of data to walk Carol through. Carol keeps saying "next, next, next," with each slide, and each time she does, Dan stops her to discuss points Carol clearly doesn't want to hear. He refuses to let Carol rush through the slides, despite the fact that Carol is clearly not interested. Dan leaves without the decision he wanted, and Carol shortens his time on the calendar for their next meeting. Once again Dan has failed to influence Carol in the way he wanted and instead moved himself further away from his desired outcome.*

*As Dan leaves the meeting, a peer asks, "How often does that 'next' thing happen?" and Dan goes on a rant about how it happens every single time and how the @\*&! CEO is making irrational decisions.*

The CEO isn't the only person being irrational here. If the way Dan is presenting the data isn't working—if this happens every time—why keep presenting the information in the same way? It doesn't make sense. Dan can't change the CEO with his data. Dan can change how he presents the data so he has a better chance of getting what he wants.

This scenario happens all day, every day: We make it painful for people to listen to us, then we get mad when they don't listen. This approach may give us something to complain about at the bar after work, but it sure spends a lot of energy for little result.

> *The next time Dan meets with Carol, he presents a deck that is distilled information rather than a sea of data. He hands Carol a clicker and lets her drive through it. This takes three minutes. Carol asks a few questions and seems more curious about the information Dan is presenting, and she is listening more than she has in the past. Encouraged, Dan says, "We have three options here . . ." and goes over the options. They argue over them and Dan doesn't get everything he wants, yet he does get movement in the right direction. He plans his next meeting with Carol based on what he's now learned about how she listens.*

### The goal of most conversation is to increase listening, yet do you do any of the following?

- Talk in a way that makes them not want to listen.
- Try to get them to listen the way *we* listen.
- They don't listen because they do not listen like you do, and you're not adapting to accommodate them.
- You blame them for not listening and walk away.

What you want doesn't happen. Doesn't make sense, does it? At this point, CEOs tell me that it is their employees' job to listen. Sure. Yet frankly, most employees get to choose their level of engagement, attention, and whether they are committed to something or are merely compliant. If you believe this to be true, the focus of any leader in influence should be to communicate for commitment rather than for compliance. Thus, it does matter **how** a leader communicates the message.

---

### Here is an example of a CEO communicating in a preference and getting less of what he wants because of it:

---

*Joe, the CEO of a Specialty Wheels & Rims company, needs his team to give the customer wow experiences. He spends a lot of money on training, development, and wall posters that focus everyone on the customer. After a product launch, he reads the customer comments about the new product, and some of the comments are negative. He copies these comments and sends an email: "WE MUST GET OUR HEAD OUT OF THE SAND AND FOCUS ON THE CUSTOMER." The head of product gets upset and says to his team, "Someone needs to get their head out of their you-know-what."*

Joe didn't get the COMMITMENT he wanted; he merely got compliance. His team isn't activated to focus on the customer; they are more defensive about his perceived attack. If Joe has a preference that his team just do what he says, he may communicate in a way that triggers people to do less of what he says. Joe is self-sabotaging, yet he is quite defiant that folks

**should** listen to the way he talks. Joe is being irrational by talking in a way that messes with his outcome.

> *Joe can do it another way. He can send an email that says, "Hey team, congrats on the product launch, we have 87% of our customers rating us with 5 stars. It looks like we have a few very vocal customers giving us feedback (see below). Can we meet for 30 minutes so you can update me on your plans, next steps and what you need from me to convert these complaints into raving fans? Does 3 p.m. work?"*

What about this sample email is better than the first one? If the reader of an e-mail gets triggered or defensive, they are not committed to listening or improving the outcome. Even if a person "should" listen and be outcome-oriented, if they feel attacked, they can get resistant. Joe can communicate in a way that gets them active to solve the situation rather than defending why it isn't their fault.

---

### Here's another example of how we self-sabotage communication in presentations because of a preference:

---

> *Tom starts his very important presentation by thanking the audience for being there because his preference is not to forget to thank people. He does it in such a low-energy manner that the audience doesn't feel it is genuine. Tom then gives the audience a few pieces of data from his bio and talks about what he will cover in the talk. The audience members' attention wanes. He hasn't engaged them,*

*so they are losing interest fast. By the time Tom gets to the good stuff in his talk (which he left until slide 5), he has to work hard to get the energy of the room up even a little bit. He feels them becoming distracted and gets nervous. He then gets frustrated, yet he is the one who created the low energy in the first place by beginning the presentation in an uninteresting and rote way.*

Just like in a one-on-one conversation, one goal of a presentation is to gain and keep the audience's interest—so why do we so often begin presentations in a way that bores both the audience *and* the speaker? This makes your job as a speaker that much more difficult because you then have to do a lot of work to get your own energy, as well as the audience's, back up to a good level. If we begin a presentation in a way that reduces listening, we have to work hard to get the audience back. We want to begin a presentation with **interest** (more on this in Section Three, How to Apply Context Model Levels). Sadly, presenting often reduces listening brought about by our preferences or habits.

One way to increase influence is to be flexible enough to notice how much preferences are driving influence around us. In the example with Joe the CEO, his preference is to be able to direct people's attention to the customer by using startling statements. Yet, if his preference isn't leading to the result he wants, he must mix it up. In the previous example, when Tom thanks the team for its hard work and offers himself as part of the solution, he will find a room that is more likely to be committed to the customer. That is just how humans work.

Are you Joe?

What are your preferences? Do you listen only to people who are like you?

What are their preferences? Are you talking in a way they cannot hear? Is that rational? Is it getting you what you want?

## People have habits that reduce listening and understanding in so much of communication.

We all have habits that reduce listening and understanding—and we just keep doing them. We live in our heads; we spend a lot of time thinking about our side of a conversation rather than noticing how (or whether) the other person is listening. When we have someone we want to influence, we often skip the most important step: being curious about the other person and what that person cares about. We say things that get us less of what we ultimately want: influence.

## Influence is a deliberate practice of curiosity and flexibility.

In the examples in this chapter where influence was reduced, the key element is that the influencer is being reactive rather than curious and open. Curiosity is a deliberate practice that, when applied, will make the model work better.

A Deliberate Practice

Pick one or two people you want to influence who are necessary for you to achieve a desired outcome. For the next few weeks, notice their preferences. What makes them listen? Avoid harshly judging their preferences as wrong; just notice the preferences. After just a week or so, can you be more flexible in how you communicate with them so you are meeting their preferences?

# What makes the person I want to influence listen more? What makes them check out?

# Chapter Four

# Invest in Two Basic Needs that Drive Influence

**People have needs; to influence a person, an investment in basic needs is a rational practice.**

Each of us has an intricate system of levers and pulleys that dictate how we listen, and each person's system is different. Most of us share two basic, fundamental truths about influence:

> *People have a basic need to feel understood.*
> *and*
> *How people feel about themselves*
> *around you impacts influence.*

**Influence is not only based on how we talk but also on how we listen and how we make people feel understood.**

When I invest in "how people feel about themselves" when they are around us, they are more likely to listen. We often make those investments when we truly **listen** to another person.

Truly helping people feel understood is a complicated, life-long practice. Remember Joe the CEO with the snarky email from the previous chapter? His email made the product team feel small so team members resisted his ideas. In the second example, he invested in how they felt about themselves and set up a meeting so they could feel understood: "What are your ideas and what do you need from me?"

Do you see how this shift in attitude can keep the group open to the outcome Joe wants?

## Humans have a basic need to feel understood.

When we listen to understand, we are filling a basic human need. We may even be giving the people we are speaking with a feeling they don't get anywhere else: the feeling of being seen and understood.

Being curious about people is a major leap toward meeting their need to feel understood. And if *you* want to feel understood, you also have to first understand others. Even so, we often do not take other people's feelings into account. At our core we do care, although in moments when we could influence people if we just showed that care, we fail to do so.

We often act in ways that ensure the need to be understood isn't met.

If we ignore people's need to be understood and to participate in the conversation, we ruin some potential to influence them. Let's use an example and instead listen to understand:

In the forgotten-wine example from Chapter One when Tim shrieks, "You ALWAYS forget stuff!", what if Susie had stopped and said, "I'm sorry, Tim. You have been here making this amazing dinner and I had one thing to do for tonight and I botched it. I'm sorry." This response may have satisfied Tim's need to feel understood and how he feels about himself.

**When we practice behaviors that help others feel understood and we improve how they feel about themselves, we will likely increase our influence.**

---

### Here is an example of how Tim and Susie could influence, using feelings:

---

(This is an example from an earlier chapter. Here I am showing you what could happen instead.)

Tim: *You ALWAYS DO THAT!*

Susie: *I know. I'm sorry. This sucks. You spent the entire day creating a magical dinner for us and I forgot the wine.*

Tim: *I'm SORRY MEANS YOU STOP DOING IT!!!*

Susie: *It does. I know (stops talking, lets him keep spewing).*

Tim: *I HAD THE WORST DAY TODAY AND YOU DON'T EVEN CARE. EVEN THOUGH I AM TRYING TO GET MY BUSINESS OFF THE GROUND, I GAVE UP ALL THE STUFF I NEEDED TO DO TO COOK YOU FREAKING DINNER. THE LEAST YOU CAN DO IS DO WHAT YOU SAY YOU ARE GOING TO DO. AND I HAD MY BIGGEST CLIENT THREATEN TO LEAVE TODAY BECAUSE MY PARTNER DIDN'T FOLLOW UP AND I DON'T KNOW WHAT TO DO ABOUT THAT. I AM SICK AND TIRED OF PEOPLE NOT DOING WHAT THEY SAY THEY WILL DO!!!*

Susie: *Oh no! Tell me about it. Can I help?*

Tim: *Well, you could have helped by getting me drunk tonight but NOOOOO . . .*

They laugh a little. Tensions reduce. They start to strategize on how to keep the client. Perhaps the yelling wasn't about the wine after all.

A few strategies in this example help with influence.

## To invest in the basic needs of being understood and how people feel about themselves around you:

Get specific rather than general.

Listen to understand rather than to respond:
Listen to understand what the person is feeling. Practice it. Let the person talk and tell you. Seek understanding, not responding.

Ask the person to tell you more: Often we respond before we actually know what the person means.

Asking someone to tell us more fills the person's need to feel understood and gives us important data. (This practice will be critical in applying the forthcoming model.)

Have empathy and compassion.
Be curious while allowing how you feel about how the person feels. We invest in influence when we simply acknowledge a feeling for a moment. Let someone be upset.

Avoid acting in a way that makes the person feel small.
When we demean someone, it is the natural human reaction to resist us.

Think about your desired outcome and how to get there.

Thinking about your desired outcome can give you perspective, unplug you from the charge of a situation, and help you take a moment to listen and think about different ways to communicate.

### If someone is yelling, it is a good time to help the person feel understood.

If someone is yelling at me, screw him—it is my right to yell back. Sure. And often we do not feel we have time for the above steps. Go back to Tim and Susie—what is the ultimate outcome we want? If it is to have a magical dinner with our spouse, doesn't it make sense that letting him emote is part of that equation? If we are in giraffe mode (it is all about ourselves), we will see that moment as a problem instead of a step toward the outcome.

---

### Here is an example of a CEO reacting rather than listening to understand:

---

*Madison is a CEO of a Specialty Shampoo company. Her head of creative is the most talented person she has ever seen. She can take a bland idea and turn it into something compelling. In an executive meeting, this head of creative says, "I just can't work like this. The rework is maddening and stupid." Madison responds, "Listen, you just have to learn to work with other people."*

Does Madison truly understand exactly what her head of creative is talking about? No. She **responded** rather than understood. Within that moment is information Madison can use to move her company forward, yet she cut it off.

We will come back to this example after we show you the model. There is another way to listen to understand.

## Influence is an investment in people.

When I watch people argue, I take a lot of mental notes. Conflict, in my view, can be a beautiful thing—sometimes we just need to do it differently. Heated moments of conflict cause us to forget we should care about what another person is saying.

## We aren't curious enough when it matters most.

Being curious about other people and investing in them will help me influence them. I may know what I want to communicate to someone, yet what if this isn't the right time or the right way to say it?

Simply being curious about other people will orient you in the proper context for any interaction.

## Influencing for commitment vs. compliance is a powerful practice.

One reason we don't ask questions is that we don't like the answers.

Curiosity and an investment in the other person's basic needs can influence commitment. Yet, we often communicate in ways that create compliance rather than commitment.

Here are some examples of compliance rather than commitment:

- There is a sign that reads "Your Mother Doesn't Work Here" in the break room, yet the sink is still filled with dishes.

- You ask your team to be on time, yet folks are often five minutes late to meetings.
- You drag your spouse to an event and it is clear she doesn't want to be there.
- By the third day of boot camp, often 50% of the attendees are absent.
- People nod in meetings yet do not do what they said they would do.

True influence means we help people find *themselves* in what we are asking so they are committed, not merely compliant. Getting commitment instead of compliance is a crucial step in attaining shared outcomes and getting desired results.

### The goal of a conversation is to increase listening, understanding, and retention.

Why? Because increased listening and understanding equals increased influence. It doesn't make sense that we talk in ways that reduce listening and influence and then blame people for not listening. *We* are the ones who own interest in the situation, after all. If my goal is to get people to listen, I should be willing to do *anything* to get them to hear me—and paying attention to *how* they listen is a good start.

### In the Joe example in Chapter Three, is he being rational?

Joe, the CEO of an accounting software company, will complain to people that his product team isn't doing what he suggests rather than change his own behavior to inspire them to do what he suggests.

This is not rational. The product team should do what he is saying; yet if they aren't, complaining about it is a waste of time. The CEO must figure out how to make this situation work FOR him rather than happen TO him; otherwise he isn't being a rational leader.

The goals in any conversation must be to increase listening, understanding and the listener's interest. If you truly want to influence, investing in how your listener receives the influence is rational. Too often we try to convince people to agree with us *before* they feel we are hearing them and understanding their perspective.

Listening is not a "step." It is a practice. If we listen to someone only for a moment and then dive in, it's not effective because it disrupts the feeling of being understood. Curiosity is the basic foundation for influence. We must be truly curious about the other people, what they care about, their perspectives, and how they listen if we want to get anywhere with them.

Let's get real here: I am not saying you need to be fascinated by everyone you talk to; I am only trying to reach your rational mind. If you truly want to influence people, you have to reduce anonymity and cultivate understanding of their patterns of listening. You have to be curious. That's what this book is about.

What we are about to show you is a tool you can apply to influence. Before we use a tool, however, being open and keeping the other person open as long as possible must be the goal. That is why the chapters so far have been focused on helping your operating system be more open so when you do use the tool, it doesn't feel like a trick or a weapon to get what you want.

## A Deliberate Practice

Think of someone you want to influence. For the next few weeks, have some non-transactional conversations with that person. Invest in how she feels about herself and her basic need to feel understood. Be curious about her as an individual and make sure not every conversation has an Ask or a Task in it. Let her talk a little more than usual.

# Am I investing in this person's basic need to feel understood by listening more?

# Section Two

# A Simple Concept that Shows Up in Most Conversations

The previous section spotlighted the reality of influence and communication. People do not understand one another as often as they should. It doesn't make sense to blame other people for not listening when it is often the way we are talking that is the real problem.

This section describes a model you can use to increase your influence. This model can help you change your way of talking and listening so you can get closer to the outcomes you want. One of the goals of communication is to increase understanding. When we focus on how we say things and how people listen rather than just on what we are saying, we are more likely to be heard and understood.

As you read this section, apply the model to how we listen and how we talk, both opportunities for influence.

# Chapter Five

# The Context Model

**People speak at varying levels of context.**

What is context?

con·text[1]

käntekst

*Noun*

1. the circumstances that form the setting for an event, statement, or idea, and in terms of which it can be fully understood and assessed:

"The decision was taken within the context of planned cuts in spending."

*synonyms:* circumstances, conditions, factors, state of affairs, situation, background, scene, setting

2. the parts of something written or spoken that immediately precede and follow a word or passage and clarify its meaning:

"Word processing is affected by the context in which words appear."

---

1   *Oxford Dictionary*

When you describe something, you can describe it at different levels of detail—you most likely heard about this in your fourth-grade writing class. People verbally establish that context in different ways—some are more abstract, others more specific. We all have habits we engage in more often than others as well as habits we engage in when we are physiologically triggered—for example, when we feel angry or frustrated.

## Here Is an Empty Visual of the Context Model:

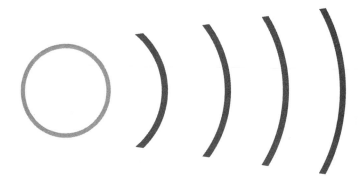

There is what we are specifically meaning (the circle) and there is the degree of abstractness to which we can describe it.

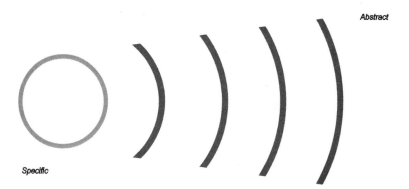

**First, let's look at a moderate level of context. We'll use fruit as an example.**

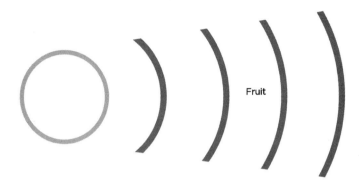

**If we want to get more general, we can describe the fruit as a food.**

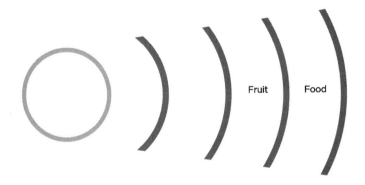

**If we want to get even more general, we can describe the food as sustenance.**

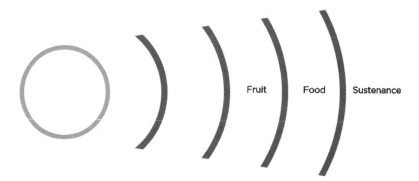

**You'll notice that on the context scale, as we get more and more general, we also get more and more abstract.**

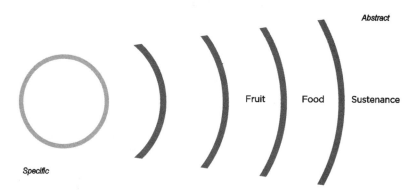

**There is a word that describes abstract words used in a corporate context:**
**Buzzwords**

These words are shortcuts that often do not really mean anything—yet we use them and think we have communicated something when we haven't. (Note: I am not saying **do not** use buzzwords. I am saying to accept that they exist. Later I'll tell you how to use them.)

If you work in a corporate setting, you may have played the game in meetings called "Buzzword Bingo."

# BUZZWORD BINGO

| DEEP DIVE | INNOVATIVE | BEST PRICE | ASAP | BOTTOM LINE |
|---|---|---|---|---|
| LEVERAGE | GROWTH HACKING | EXPERT | ACTIONABLE | QUALITY |
| INTEGRITY | SCALE | ⭐ | SYNERGY | INTERAC-TIVE |
| OPTIMIZE | MISSION CIRTICAL | PARADIGM SHIFT | COLLABORA-TION | POWER SHIFT |
| INTEGRATE | NIMBLE | EMPOWER | VELOCITY | STRATEGIC |

In this comical game, whoever catches the buzzwords in a row wins a beer. Although fun, this game points to how ineffective buzzwords can be in driving understanding.

Some buzzwords you might hear a lot in the corporate world include:

- deep dive
- synergy
- growth hacking
- paradigm shift
- integrity
- quality
- best price
- ASAP
- Velocity

If buzzwords are shortcuts that *sound* important but often don't mean anything, then it stands to reason that when someone is talking at buzzword level, we often *think* we understand when we actually don't.

---

## An example of buzzwords creating miscommunication:

---

*Joe tells Carol, "Have this done ASAP"—so Carol cancels a client meeting to get it done. When she sends it to Joe, he is impressed that she was able to get it done and meet with the client. When he finds out she canceled the meeting, he gets upset. "You said as soon as possible," Carol says. "That means right away, drop everything!" Joe replies, "No, it doesn't. It means when you have a spare moment."*

**Buzzwords can be a buzzkill.**

Because you can't sway people if you're not sure they understand you, empty buzzwords do not always drive behavior. Still, people use them. We will come back to this in a moment; let's see how this model plays out.

**If we want to stop using buzzwords, we must be more specific.**

### Apple

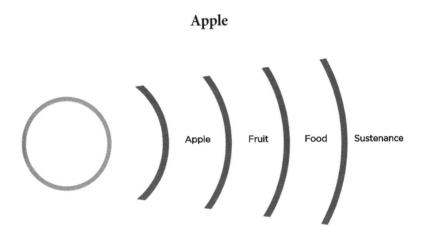

If we were in a room together having this conversation, I'd ask you to shout out the name of a type of fruit.

When I do this in presentations, someone yells out "apple!" more than half the time.

I chuckle a bit when this happens, because "apple" is also a computer brand—which sort of proves how easy it is to miscommunicate without context. In this example, we know we're talking about a fruit, so we get what the person is saying. Yet without the model in front of you, you can see how easy it would be to misunderstand what the person means.

**We can be even more specific by telling what *kind* of apple.**

### Granny Smith Apple

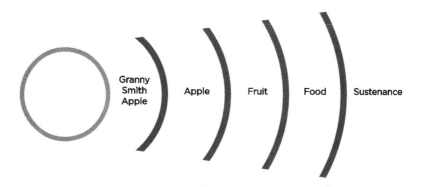

Even more specific than an apple is a Granny Smith apple. We are getting more detailed now, to the point that most folks may have an image. Instead of putting forth the concept of an apple, which would have everyone thinking of a different type—red, yellow perhaps—most of us who have heard "Granny Smith" will have the image of a small, bright green, tart and tangy apple visualized. The difference in what type of apple we should be thinking about can matter in some circumstances.

---

### Here is a silly example of how context could matter:

---

*Which apple would you pick if you had the* context *that it would be used in a photo shoot depicting a scene from* Snow White? *Which apple would you pick if you had the* context *that it would be used to bake a pie?*

By being more specific, we are more likely to get the thing we really want.

We have also increased mindshare by using a more specific example.

*Mindshare,* the way I am describing it, is a **vivid** moment in the brain that tends to last a bit longer or stays longer. Each of us has a finite amount of things we can think about and remember. The things that are most vivid seem to take up much of the share of space in our head, our mindshare. By our speaking at the Granny Smith level of context, due to a vivid visual the listener becomes more engaged, more involved in what we are saying, and more likely to be thinking of what we *mean* to say rather than what we *meant* to say. The more specific a concept is, the more the influencer creates the image they wish the person to remember.

**A Granny Smith apple, although more vivid than just saying "apple," still is missing some context.**

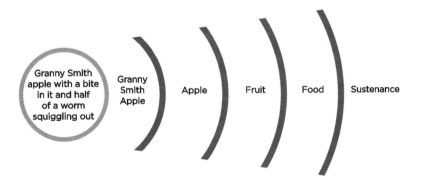

*"A green Granny Smith apple with a bite taken out of it; half
a worm is squiggling out of the core (implying that you have the
rest of the worm in your mouth)."*

*Ewww . . .*

The stuff in the circle is **specifically** what we are referring
to.

**There is a major difference between a yummy Granny
Smith apple and a Granny Smith apple with a worm
in it.**

Folks typically cringe when I talk about half a worm. Did
you experience an *ick* moment? Specific level of context often
has a feeling or emotion connected with it.

I believe this is why we often use buzzwords and vague
communication. There is less experiential conflict if I just tell
my team we need to have more velocity, rather than getting
specific.

---

### Let's look at an example of the model in a business setting:

---

A CEO, *Jill, tells her Medical Device company,*
*"We must increase velocity."*

She could be using the word *velocity* to avoid
specific conflict. Most can agree with the idea of
velocity as an idea; it is in the practice that things
get hard. To reach velocity, I have to make some
deliberate tradeoffs that result in conflict and disagreement. She may think she is rallying a room
with her **velocity** comment when she actually may
be confusing or disconnecting from the room. (Of
course there are exceptions wherein a rallying cry

at an abstract level of context is still effective.) She could have said, "We can make the ship date if we make these two deliberate tradeoffs, get with your teams and . . ." This is velocity at a more specific level of context.

The more we generalize, the less effectively we are describing what we are talking about.

Hey, are you absorbing right now, or are you still stuck on a sentence in the preceding paragraph? I mean the one that says CEOs may use the word *velocity* to avoid specific conflict. That was a broad, sweeping statement and not entirely true. It was provocative, and I take it back. CEOs often use broad, sweeping statements to save time and to broadcast what they are trying to say, not realizing that the generalization can cause low action or change. More on this later. For now, just know that sometimes we generalize to save time, sometimes to avoid conflict, and sometimes because we really do not have anything specific to say. When do you generalize? Is it working for you?

If you think about the graphic, the less descriptive we are, the further we are from direct, specific action or example. That isn't always a bad thing, just something to be aware of as we are designing our communication.

So, that's basically it. It is straightforward in concept, yet the nuance of how to make it come alive takes practice.

## We can all be a bit more deliberate in how we communicate.

We often speak in ways that let the other person decide what we meant to describe. However, with a little bit of practice, we can communicate what it is we are really trying to say. This requires more upfront energy, but it will pay off. My belief is that we spend less time in the aggregate when we communicate by design rather than by default.

A Deliberate Practice

Listen for levels of context. If someone asks you to do something, notice how specific the request is. If you are directing someone to do something, notice if you are being specific enough about what it is you are asking for.

## Am I being specific?

# Chapter Six

# Use the Model as a General Practice

**Levels of context are used in the way you *talk* and the way you *listen*.**

*How this model impacts you and your ability to influence:*

Most of us have habits around how we use context. We may be very general with instructions yet specific in feedback. I notice that I get vague when I'm tired or not really engaged.

Creating a habit around noticing and using context to increase influence takes practice. If we can LISTEN for what level of context a conversation is in, we can then decide if the context we are in is increasing influence or not.

Using context is the one habit that seems to be challenging for people to master. For some reason, some people seem to ignore the very existence of specific context. In the previous chapter I gave you a general example of how a CEO may stumble using a buzzword; here I make that vague example even more specific in the hope it creates more clarity for you.

## An example of a CEO's general request not changing behavior:

*Jack, a CEO, stands up in front of his team at an all-staff meeting. He wants to inspire the room to behave differently and to solve an organizational challenge that he sees as impacting both morale and execution. Jack is earnest and truly wants to help, and in his impassioned speech he asks the team to "increase velocity." At the end of the talk, he gets the obligatory applause, yet nothing really changes. In fact,* velocity *becomes a word people use against one another as a weapon when they are upset; not only does it fail to create positive change, it has a negative impact.*

Context matters. Exhorting his employees to "increase velocity" without explaining what that means can come off like a complaint or an attack. It's too abstract. It doesn't make people feel seen for the work they are doing or instruct them how to make the desired improvements. An abstract request can drive an equally abstract response.

For example, after requesting velocity, the CEO might hear, "Well, you can't have quality and speed at the same time, so which one do you want?" Or, maybe people will leave the meeting and just walk faster—that's a type of velocity, after all.

If Jack really wants more velocity, he needs to help his team get closer to the *action* he actually wants. Imagine if instead of saying "increase velocity" he said, "We can ship three weeks earlier if we make these two deliberate tradeoffs." Rainbows and unicorns storm into the meeting and everyone is happy, right? Um, nope.

The reality is, some folks won't agree with the specifics Jack sets forth. That is where things get good! More on that later; for now, just know the story doesn't end with the specific statement. This is where conflict happens, and most organizations need specific conflict rather than complaint conflict.

**Context (specificity or examples) helps people understand what you mean.**

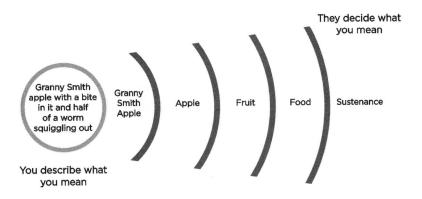

Look at the model. When we are vague, the other person gets to decide what we mean. When we are more specific, especially if we use an example, we describe what we mean. At this level things make a little more sense, but it is also often where conflict happens. Sometimes we give an example, they defend, we fight, and nothing changes. Yet, there are times when we give an example and they know what to change.

We sometimes avoid detail to avoid controversy, and yet when we avoid detail, we fail to communicate our needs clearly (which can lead to our anger because what we want isn't executed). When I mediate conflict, I frequently find that the "ask" was never clear.

## An example of an unclear ask:

*Gwyneth asks her husband, Frank, if he is all set to make dinner tonight for their family. He says yes. Gwyneth gets home to find Frank and the kids eating sugar cereal for dinner and is furious that he didn't make something healthier, as she would have done. She could have gotten more context from him or given him more context about what she expects a proper dinner to include, like protein and vegetables.*

## An example of lack of context resulting in misunderstood next steps:

*In Brad's annual review of Janet, he says, "Basically, Janet, you just need to work on your communication."*

*Janet leaves thinking she needs to keep more people in the loop on what she's doing, so she creates a plan to email everyone more often. She also assumes this is about the challenge she keeps having with Magenta in accounting, and that she needs to improve that relationship. Brad, meanwhile, sits back in his chair, relieved that Janet is going to email less from now on. He is so tired of the constant inbox spam from her.*

**Far too often we talk in a context that is too abstract to create action.**

---

## Think about the example again. What the heck could "work on your communication" possibly mean?

---

Does Janet talk too much, too little, too loudly? Does she email too much or too little? Does she talk so quickly it feels like a time warp? Does she shy away from conflict too much? Does she need to learn to listen better? Brad isn't offering enough detail for Janet to identify the action she needs to take.

Brad needs to use the context scale to help Janet know exactly what she needs to change. (See Chapter Ten for more specific how-to.) Janet, meanwhile, needs to take the initiative and ask for more details from Brad. Why would she leave his office before asking exactly what he wants her to change?

**As listeners, it is also our responsibility to ask for examples and specificity rather than assuming we know.**

Context isn't just in what we **say**; we must also **listen** for context as well. Do we know what the person is telling us or is it too vague to know what to do?

People have their own definitions of what your context means.

The challenge with context is that it can be very personal and based on individual experiences and preferences. We may think we are communicating to be understood, yet in the rush of day-to-day conversations, we are often communicating in a way that is vague and can be interpreted another way.

People remember what is most vivid and specific, yet we often talk in ways that are not memorable or understandable.

What was the percentage in the beginning of this little book? I find that most folks remember that silly number, even though it is entirely made up. I even told you I made it up, yet you may have remembered the number because it was a detail and increased mindshare.

## There is no silver bullet or *right* level of context.

One person may need more detail and another may exclaim when things get too detailed: "Don't bring a fire hose when what you really need is an eyedropper." Sigh.

Learning to play on the context scale requires a **curiosity** around how individuals listen and understand. For some, a lot of context makes them listen more. For others, it impedes their desire to listen. You will need to practice **noticing** and being **curious** about what level of context works for the person you are influencing, including asking questions.

Context has two verbs: how you *talk* and how you *listen*. We can use the levels of context in both acts of communication.

## Here is an example that just happened in this book:

There is a percentage of readers who giggled a little at the Brad, Janet and Magenta example above. Why? The names are specific to a movie from the late 70s called *Rocky Horror Picture Show* where there was a dance called the Time Warp. Using those specific names could have increased interest in a reader, while others just thought our name choice was weird. The challenge with context is there is no right level that will work with everyone and every situation. Context is a deliberate *practice* to increase understanding and outcomes.

### Notice what level of context you are in and if it is working for your physiology.

You'll also want to notice what level of context you use that *isn't* helping you communicate physiologically. What I mean is this: You may be someone who gets bored by speeches that begin with buzzwords and generalities. You may be someone who *loves* buzzwords. A detail can either increase or decrease listening.

---

### Here is a silly example referencing a specific detail from the past:

---

*You may be someone who is still upset that Wham! broke up, and you remember what you were wearing on the day you found out. You may be someone who has no idea who Wham! is, and I have just outed my age group. If you hated Wham!, I may have just triggered your preferences.*

Whether or not you know Wham!, my referencing it causes your physiology to activate toward something: memory, confusion, curiosity, preference, nostalgia; the possibilities are endless. And therein lies a lot of influence. Getting people to feel anything about something is a start to gaining their attention and understanding. Yet it can also **repulse** them, and this is why I think we habitually talk in generalities. We give up understanding to avoid negative reactions. This is not a good strategy.

Here is an example of a CEO using *context* and curiosity to improve outcomes. Remember the story from an earlier chapter about Madison the CEO reacting to a statement?

*Madison is a CEO. Her head of creative is the most talented person she has ever seen. She can take a bland idea and turn it into something compelling. In an executive meeting, this head of creative says, "I just can't work like this. The rework is maddening and stupid." Madison responds, "Listen, you just have to learn to work with other people."*

Does Madison truly understand exactly what her head of creative is talking about? No. She responded rather than understood. Within that moment, there is information Madison can use to move her company forward, yet she cut it off.

Now, let's have the CEO use this situation to drive outcomes. Applying the Context Model, watch her *listen to understand:*

*Head of Creative: "I just can't work like this. The rework is maddening and stupid."*

*Madison: "Oh no. Tell me what happened . . ."*

*Head of Creative: "The founder keeps calling meetings with my team a couple of days before launch telling them our stuff is crap and to redo it."*

*Madison: "That is hard. I want to help; are you open to my help here?"*

*HOC: "That is why I am telling you; make him stop the rework."*

*Madison: "I am here to help. Let's take one specific launch and walk through the timeline. How much input did the founder give prior to the last meeting?"*

*HOC: "None. We reveal the product to the founder toward the end of the process."*

*Madison: "Ah-ha! Our founder creates the best ideas when he is editing other ideas rather than creating from thin air. It is how his genius works. To avoid rework and to get the most from his genius, how about we road test an idea? How about we include him in these two meetings—and let's call them* ideation *meetings. Then, two weeks prior to final, include me in the meeting with the founder for the final road test. We will all agree on go/no go and get his agreement that if he doesn't say no in the next 24 hours it is a go. I think the extra pressure will help him do what he does best, create disruptive ideas. How does this sound?"*

*HOC: "Can you tell me more about the first part: He edits rather than creates?"*

*Madison: "Yes, this is his genius. Let me explain a little more and we will work together to improve . . ."*

In this example, the CEO helped discover **why** the feeling of rework was happening, and it was because of **when** the founder was included in the process. Had the CEO became reactive and told Madison to just "buck up butter cup," they would not have discovered there was another way to deploy the Founder in the creative timeline. The conflict wasn't about getting along with people; the real crux of it was when to deploy the genius of another person to get the best outcomes. The more a leader can facilitate a confrontation toward a conversation, the more likely the situation can be improved.

Use the Context Model to liberate solutions by using examples.

## Context helps people listen and sometimes triggers people not to listen.

Eek. So what is a person to do? Go back to Section One and be flexible enough to shift what you are doing so you can increase listening and understanding.

## Notice what level of context the person you're talking to is using and if you understand what is meant.

---

### Here is an example in which missing context could result in incorrect action at work:

---

*Jan's boss emails her. "Jan, the client's flight comes in at 11. Please have someone pick her up at SFO Airport, United."*

*Jan looks at her watch and sees it is 10 a.m. She sends her assistant, Chuck, to the airport that is 45 minutes away. She walks away a little frustrated by the last-minute request.*

*Chuck doesn't act right away. Instead, he asks Jan for the flight number and the name of the client. His plan is to make sure the flight is on time and to get the cell phone number from the client record just in case of delays. Jan gets annoyed and says, "I do not have the flight number; it is Joe Smythe of ABC. You need to get in the car right now if you want to make it."*

*Chuck could jump in the car, yet he stops to get a little more context. He realizes Jan is in a bad mood and decides not to ask her for more details. Instead, Chuck calls the client's assistant and she gives him all the details. It turns out the flight comes in at 11 p.m. Chuck sets up a car service, gives all the details to the client's assistant, and goes on about his day.*

Context made sure the desired outcome happened. Context does get humans closer to understanding; yet sometimes if a person is unwilling to give us details we have to figure out how to get what we need on our own. Getting curious rather than frustrated helps us get the outcomes we want more effectively.

## Buzzwords aren't always something to avoid.

Converting a buzzword into details is a good practice. Often, however, folks believe I am saying NEVER to use buzzwords. That is not what I am saying. If people you are trying to influence use certain buzzwords often, notice what buzzwords they tend to use and make sure you use those words when describing your ideas to them.

When we communicate with people using our own favorite words, they may not be able to find themselves in what we are saying. Yet if we translate our details into *their* favorite words, we have a much greater chance of getting our points across.

### Here is an example of using a buzzword to increase an individual's listening:

*Ken has been trying to convince Kendra, the CEO of his company, to allow employees to Tweet at events without the Brand team doing oversight. He often talks about how the approval is onerous and bureaucratic. He isn't getting what he wants. So, for the next few meetings, he pays special attention to what Kendra talks about and notices she often repeats the phrase "We need to disrupt ourselves." In Ken's next presentation he includes a slide that says, "Disruptive thinking has a very short window." Suddenly, Kendra is listening. She asks questions and then approves event Tweeting. Ken is shocked. Was it really that easy?*

In this case, it was. Ken had been making things difficult for himself by trying to force Kendra to see a larger problem of bureaucracy. When he started framing his "ask" with what she cared about, there was more of a chance she'd listen.

## To influence another person, we must influence *the way* people are influenced.

One concept that may help this chapter make more sense is the idea of "Cognitive Illusions," an idea first suggested in the nineteenth century by Hermann von Helmholtz.

What is a cognitive illusion? A quick web search says, "Cognitive illusions are assumed to be interactions based on assumptions about the world, which lead to unconscious inferences."

Well, those are a lot of words that make my head hurt.

Here is my take: The human brain takes in a lot of information. To deal with the data onslaught, we have shortcuts that can give us misinformation. Folks with commas and degrees after their names call these shortcuts cognitive illusions.

Still a bit confusing? Our brains shortcut information and thus can often misinterpret stuff. The examples (context) below may make cognitive illusions make a bit more sense.

Levels of context can play with or into these illusions, of which there are many. For the purpose of this book we will address only two of them:

### The mind remembers what is most vivid. Being detailed can increase retention.

We often try to influence people with generic information. When we use more specific details, we may create mind-share and at least get people to see in their minds what we are talking about. Sometimes being more vivid increases the chance a person will remember what we said. If I use a detail about an odd object in a story, you may think of me when you see that specific object again. (For example, a Granny Smith apple is more vivid than a plain apple and thus is a bit more memorable.)

We can either **describe** what we mean or let someone else **decide** what we mean.

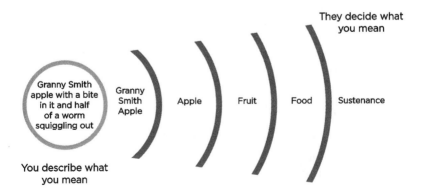

They decide what you mean

Granny Smith apple with a bite in it and half of a worm squiggling out

Granny Smith Apple

Apple

Fruit

Food

Sustenance

You describe what you mean

If we communicate in a way that is more **vivid** or increases mindshare, we may engage the person. If we do engage, that person is listening. Using **vivid** communication can increase retention.

## We see what we already believe.

In other words, we see the things we are looking for.

Using or asking for details increases understanding. Humans make a lot of assumptions, and specifics can reduce misunderstandings. (In the case of Brad and Janet, Janet's belief is that lots of emails mean better communication, so that is what she believes he is talking about.)

(For a deeper dive into cognitive illusions, see *Cognitive Illusions: A Handbook on Fallacies and Biases in Thinking, Judgment and Memory,* edited by Rüdiger F. Pohl. Psychology Press, 2004.)

## A Deliberate Practice

The next time you walk outside, look for a white Prius. You will likely notice more of them now that you are looking for them. We see what we are looking for and what is vivid. Notice how vivid you are being when you want folks to remember something.

After you do that practice, here is another that may improve your physiology with someone you have to influence who also bugs you:

Think of the label you have when you think about

her. Look for the *opposite* of that label in her for three weeks. You may feel your physiology ease up around her.


## *Can I look for the opposite of any label I have so I see more of the reality?*

# Chapter Seven

# Abstract Choices May Mess with Outcomes

**Conflict often exists in specificity, and if we do not like conflict, we will be vague.**

Before I give you more specific examples, I need to speak to your open, rational mind. We often get a little binary when we hear things like what I'm about to tell you. By *binary* I mean that we see things as **either/or** or **black/white**.

**As you read, ask yourself if you ever avoided specificity for these reasons:**

1. **Detailed context often creates or contains emotion.**

When we explain with examples, we feel things—and feelings can make us act weird. I find that in business specifically, folks spend a fair amount of energy numbing their emotions because they don't want to be thought of as professionals who can't control themselves.

Emotions exist, and numbing them requires effort. That effort can be exhausting. So, we use buzzwords and generalities to keep the emotions from taking over, so that:

- we do not tear up.
- we do not appear bitter or angry.
- we do not get other people upset or angry.
- we do not create controversy we then will have to deal with.
- we do not make the meeting last longer because people don't agree with our version of "velocity."

Instead of avoiding emotions, we can celebrate them. By using specific levels of context, you may find that you have a lot more little conversations rather than big, hairy conversations built on pent-up conflict.

## 2.  Detailed context can create conflict.

When we are abstract, it is hard for anyone to disagree with us. Specifics are what cause people to become offended or defensive.

---

### Here is an example of a CEO trying to get his team to have a new behavior but failing to be specific:

---

*A CEO asks his executive team to collaborate more. Everyone nods. If we interview all the executive members after the meeting and ask what they think the CEO meant, each points to someone else as the one who isn't collaborating. All the executives think the CEO was talking about someone other than themselves.*

*I bring everyone back in the next day and force them to 'fess up about their belief that the CEO was talking about someone else. I've coached the CEO to be more example-based in his feedback; he looks each person in the eye and says specifically how he feels that person has not been collaborating. People get offended and defensive. Some shut down; others fight back, trying to clarify what has actually happened.*

*It takes two hours. Faces get red. Folks get uncomfortable. It is not fun.*

*Then something happened. The CTO said, "The reason we do not collaborate is that we have competing priorities. We do not act as a team. If we are all willing to have a conversation about that, things will change." He looked at the CEO. "Are you willing to have a conversation about competing priorities right here and now?"*

*A heated debate ensued. At the end of the day, they made agreements as a team about what to do next and how to keep collaboration an action rather than an idea. This team went on to dismiss one of the executives who refused to be more collaborative and ultimately succeeded in achieving the vision they'd agreed upon.*

---

## Let's spend a moment thinking about how to apply the Context Model to the previous example:

---

An executive team runs a business. Its shared outcomes are the success of the business as a whole rather than just the department. Often, executive teams will not agree on an idea or initiative. One way to think about collaboration from an executive perspective is a metaphor called "Oars out of the Water." This is a more vivid way to describe a facet of collaboration. Here's how it works:

We will not always agree. Because people like to be right, they may hold on to an old idea and will spend precious time trying to change the mind of a decider or sabotage the success of the chosen idea. The reality is that a **bad** idea can be made good if everyone makes it good and a **great** idea can be made bad if just one executive has her oars in the water and refuses to **row** or help the idea succeed. The reason one of the executives was let go for not collaborating is because she was unwilling to keep rowing if she didn't agree with the direction. She kept putting her oars in the water, so she slowed down the boat. For some, the more specific description of collaboration makes the example more clear. For others, it confuses things. This is the challenge of context: Each individual listens differently.

Yes, being specific can create conflict that is often difficult and uncomfortable to endure. Still, is it more difficult than staying general and ignoring or tolerating what it is you feel really needs to change? This is why we may speak in the abstract to avoid **real** conflict even though we can't effect real change without it.

### 3. People believe buzzwords make them succinct and save time; that is not always the case.

You don't have to be a mathematician to understand that using fewer words decreases the amount of time we spend talking. Spending less time saying what we need to say isn't the primary goal, however—creating understanding is.

If you have a boss who looks at her watch the moment you start talking, being brief may be your goal. Yet being brief doesn't have to mean using more buzzwords. What you really need to do is figure out how to get your boss to listen by removing some of the content you're trying to communicate. Better that she hears the most important parts of what you're saying than trying to give her **all** the content and ending up with her not retaining/listening/understanding any of it.

---

### Here is an example of an employee influencing a boss who doesn't listen:

---

*Caitlyn needs her boss to make a decision on the three-year strategy roll-out. Her boss, Nancy, has almost no listening bandwidth. Instead of walking through 15 decision points, Caitlyn gives her boss one clear decision that impacts the remaining 15. "In this upcoming alignment meeting, can the directors weigh in and change the strategy or is it already fully baked?" With that decision, she can select the remaining two critical decisions. She provides options for each implication.*

Caitlyn may wish her boss would listen more, yet the reality is she doesn't. So Caitlyn plans a strategy of specific, easy next steps to get to the result she wants.

Using a buzzword or a generalized complaint may save upfront speaking time, but it can make the desired **action** not happen or take longer than it needs to—unless, as we discussed earlier, you're using a buzzword you know the person loves and will respond to. The purpose of influence is to inspire some sort of action, yet we often get confused and shortcut real communication in exchange for an abstract idea that won't affect action.

### 4.  Detail forces us to verbalize deliberate tradeoffs.

Life is complicated. Because we often have to make deliberate tradeoffs that are hard decisions, we get a little reluctant to verbalize them. If the other person is really listening, verbalizing these tradeoffs can increase understanding.

---

### Here is an example of an executive not using context to verbalize tradeoffs:

---

*A CMO has a strict budget she can use to upgrade the company's retail website. The deadline is fast approaching. She has had to make some serious tradeoffs to land on time and within budget. One tradeoff is the iPad. Since less than 1% of her customers are on an iPad, she made a tradeoff to handle the iPad in a secondary launch. All the updates with the executive team go well as she explains that everything is on track. The day of the launch, though, she gets a call from the CEO, upset that the website isn't functioning. The CMO hits her forehead with her hand, realizing she'd forgotten that the CEO works only on an iPad.*

Had she verbalized the deliberate tradeoffs at a detailed level of context earlier, the confrontation would have happened sooner and would have been resolved to the CEO's satisfaction. Perhaps she would have even received more funds to update the company website.

## 5.  Humans are warm-blooded, tribal anim
### act like one another.

I'm not Jane Goodall so maybe what I just ѕ⸺
entific fact—but it really sounds true. Humans mimic one
another in organizational environments. If others are doing
something, we have a tendency to do it, too.

---
### Here is an example of how context can be seen in cultures:
---

*Susie traveled to four states in four days. She was struck by the different culture of each state. When she arrived in Doraville, Georgia, she noticed how people all seemed to flirt with one another. Strangers talked to one another in the elevator and lightly touched others' elbows when they stood in proximity and talked. The exit from the elevator was a leisurely stroll as the conversation continued. As she landed in Newark, New Jersey, Susie realized she had to walk a bit faster to keep pace with the crowd. In the elevator people stood far apart and didn't talk to one another. When she arrived in Santa Barbara, California, she heard a lot of people say "dude" and "totally" as they talked about the ocean swells that day. Their only interaction was about the weather and the ocean. As she landed home in Idaho, she was pleased to see people helping one another with their suitcases. The world around her was familiar and comfortable.*

I think it is clear to most of us that culture reflects a set of behaviors people adopt as they become a part of that culture.

People have habits, and so do organizations. One habit I have noticed in organizations is speaking at an abstract level of context.

---

### Here are two examples of abstract context at work (we mentioned the first one earlier in the book):

---

*Candy says, "I need this ASAP." As soon as possible. That seems specific, doesn't it? Well, maybe not. What she meant by ASAP is "within the next five minutes." In other words, "drop everything and do it now." Pat's meaning of ASAP is by the end of the day after he finishes his top client tasks.*

ASAP isn't descriptive enough as each person can think it means something else.

*A similar example is TMI:*

*Candy says to Pat, "TMI, man. Too much information." That seems specific, doesn't it? Well, maybe not. When she meant by TMI is "tell me in less than 30 seconds." Pat heard, "Never tell me personal stuff again." TMI isn't descriptive enough as each person can think it means something else.*

## 6. We let anger trump logic.

When we become frustrated with people, we may just want them to feel bad. In these moments, we sometimes use abstract context as an attack mechanism.

## Here is an example of levels of context being used as an attack:

*William is often late dropping off his son to his ex-wife. Ann can't remember the last time he brought little Jimmy over on time. Tonight she has dinner reservations, so after waiting 10 minutes, she calls William. "When are you going to get here?" she hisses into the phone. "You are always late."*

*When he hangs up, William is so pissed off with Ann that he drives even more slowly, deliberately making himself even later. When he finally gets to Ann's place, they have a nasty exchange. Ann loses her dinner reservation. Her anger has trumped her logic.*

What can Ann do to ensure that her ex is on time? She could tell him he needs to arrive 15 minutes earlier than he actually needs to. She could calmly and rationally explain that when he is late, it messes with her schedule. She could let him know that a call or text warning he is behind schedule would be helpful.

This example is difficult because there's never an easy solution when it comes to the dynamics between people who share an emotional history. We often can't change other people, and our attempts to change them may create more defiant resistance. The lesson here is that being abstract—as when Ann uses *always* to describe William's lateness—can feel good in the moment, but we are far more likely to get the outcome we want if we are specific.

Unless, as previously discussed, specificity doesn't work for the individual involved. That is what makes this all so freaking hard! You'll have to stay flexible and curious about your situation and the person with whom you're communicating. Notice what works and what doesn't. These are the keys to influence.

Anger isn't bad—it is just an emotion. Sometimes pushing back and setting a boundary in an angry way is exactly right. Nothing in this book should imply that anger is bad; it is a feeling to be felt. My goal in this book is to give other options or ways of moving closer to the outcome we want with either curiosity, timing or a whole list of other ways. Sometimes if someone is standing on your foot, it is okay to yell at them to get off of it.

**7.  We can get lazy when it comes to communicating.**

It takes hard work to communicate efficiently. We have to be prepared with forethought—and in some cases, research—to communicate the point we intend. To be rational, we must focus on the outcome of understanding rather than just on the transaction of speaking.

**8.  Sometimes abstract context *is* the right choice.**

- When we want other people to figure out the specifics of how to do something. Here is an example of a leader using a buzzword to do that:
  *A leader tells her team she wants "zero glitches" as an outcome, giving the team the space to decide how to make that happen.*

- When a specific person *must* hear a certain buzzword in order to activate. Here is an example of a person listening more when he hears his buzzword:

   *Carla has a boss who hates to plan and always cancels the planning meetings Carla tries to schedule. On the calendar Carla has been calling these meetings "Planning Meeting." Carla has noticed that her boss loves ideas and anything new. Whenever someone uses the buzzwords* innovate *or* idea, *Carla's boss becomes attentive. So Carla decides to change the "Planning Meeting" to a 20-minute "Ideation Meeting." It works, and Carla's boss is enthusiastic. Carla changes the tone of the meeting and gets the planning she needs through her boss's ideas.*

   *"Do you have a second to* plan *the upcoming event?"*
   vs.
   *"Let's toss around some ideas for the upcoming event."*

   If the person I am trying to influence **loathes** planning and **loves** ideas, I can translate the activity into something he likes to do. Of course, I am not telling you to use lies as a strategy. We lose influence permanently when we lie or dupe people as a strategy. Don't do it.

- As a repeated rallying chant.
   Examples: (See how many you recognize.)
   - *I'm lovin' it! (McDonald's)*
   - *Just Do It (Nike)*

- *Think Different (Apple)*
- *May the Force be with you (Star Wars)*

- If someone is emotionally charged and needs time before hearing details. Here is an example of an emotionally charged moment when perhaps it isn't the right time to give details:

  *You're late, and your boss says, "You are always late." Instead of explaining the details of bad traffic or your alarm clock breaking, you just say, "I'm sorry I'm late, and you have a right to be angry with me because it's happened before. It won't happen again."*

## A Deliberate Practice

In the list above, pick a habit you know you do. Create a deliberate practice to *notice* when you are in the habit, then look at the Context Model to shift to another way of doing things.

### *What is one influence-reducing habit I can reduce?*

# Chapter Eight

# Practice the Context Model

We've given you many examples of levels of context. What now?

**Begin by noticing.**
Over the next couple of weeks, notice the context scale around you. Create a deliberate practice to reflect on levels of context during and after conversations. **Listen** and notice what level of context is in the culture around you.

---
### Here is an example of context in an all-hands meeting:
---

*You are in a team meeting in which the entire room is unengaged and on handhelds. You notice that no one listens to your boss until she talks about a karaoke bar in Japan that requires patrons to wear fishnet stockings.*

It seems that details and stories work in this room.

---
### Here is an example of noticing it's not the right time for context:
---

*Your boss seems pretty agitated by execution*

*issues. You notice she gets angrier when people ask specific questions.*

Specific levels of context with your boss may not be an appropriate tool when she is frustrated. It may be better to ask specific questions at another time or it may be okay to be okay with her agitation and ask anyway. This example is an important and interesting one. Specific levels of context aren't some magical or universal elixir to apply to every situation; sometimes when we apply it, things will get a little uncomfortable. We can time when we use context for when the person is more open to our questions.

---

## Here is an example of noticing context in presentations:

---

*You see an incredible TED talk and stop to think about the level of context the speaker used to communicate. The entire talk was told at a very detailed and specific level of context. The parts of the presentation you liked the most were very detailed (or maybe you liked the opposite, which is also good to know).*

---

## Here is an example of noticing context in an argument:

---

*You notice your partner is angry. She is screaming at you in a very abstract way—saying that you don't care about her, yet omitting what has made her feel that way.*

Broad sweeping statements often mean the person is feeling emotional. Maybe rather than sit, notice and analyze, just practice compassion and hug her. Practice empathy.

## Tune into the *context* channel.

After tuning into the context channel for a while, you may begin to notice different levels of context. Embrace noticing as a deliberate practice.

Avoid using the Context Model as a weapon. We all have habits that work for us and ones that don't. When humans are triggered they often communicate poorly, so try to forgive others—and yourself—when this occurs.

A Deliberate Practice

Notice what level of context you like the most. Notice what others like the most.

*Can I notice Levels of Context in conversations and conflict and push for understanding?*

## Section Three

# How to Apply Context Model Levels

We get better when we practice something until it becomes a habit. In this section we give you many ways to use Context Model levels so using them will become habitual.

So you can dive a little deeper into the model's application, each chapter describes a communication skill in which the Context Model levels are useful.

Keep in mind that as you read this section, your physiology should be open and curious to its contents. If you aren't curious when you use the model, folks can feel tricked, manipulated, or managed by its application. Influence will be decreased.

# Chapter Nine

# Presentations

This chapter helps you apply the Context Model to presentations. It is set up in sections based on what makes an effective presentation:

- Your physiology while presenting
- What your audience cares about
- How the audience members feel about themselves as they listen to you
- Storytelling
- The content of your speech and your ability to make it interesting
- A specific process to improve presentations

Although random events you have no control over impact presentations—like whether Mercury is in retrograde—for the purpose of this section we will focus only on how to use the Context Model to sway an audience.

### *Your physiology matters when giving a presentation.*

## What is the physiology of presentations?

First, let's discuss physiology in speaking. When our physiology is triggered*, various physical reactions manifest:

- Dry mouth
- Shaky hands
- Nervous pacing or rocking
- Stuttering or stammering
- Low energy
- Monotone or flat speech patterns
- Forgetfulness
- Spacing out
- Feeling faint or the sensation of floating
- Blinking or squinting eyes

*Triggered* can be such a negative word. I'd rather use *activated*. A shift in our physiology (an activation) isn't necessarily bad; it is our attempt to numb that activation that turns it into a trigger. One of the tools that seems to help a lot of folks align their physiology is using the levels of context before presentations and at the beginning of them.

Many ways are available to improve your physiology. Here are some ways to use the Context Model to help your physiology be more open and work **for** you.

## Get out of your head by looking for positive detail before the presentation.

One reason speakers reduce verbal effectiveness is that right before the presentation they are in their head, thinking about their presentation. Instead, prior to speaking create a deliberate practice to get out of your head and **notice** the details of the world around you.

## Here is an example of a presenter using positive detail to improve her physiology at work:

*Nicole was worried about her presentation. The room was full of parents who were upset about the lunch program. The more she thought about the bitterness in the room and the more she tried to remember what she was going to say, the more her hands shook. She wrote down the five things she wanted to say, highlighted the three data points, and put her speaking notes on the lectern. She then walked around searching for positive detail in the room. She noticed the students helping the teachers set up the snack table. She saw parents hugging and tearing up a bit, showing community in the school. She started noticing all the types of shoes people wore and laughing at how much detail there was in the room. The more she got out of her head, the more her physiology became more comfortable. With a new ease, she went up to people she knew were super positive and asked them questions about their plans for the summer. The more detailed the conversation got, the fewer nerves she had.*

*When she opened her speech, she was able to start with a story that happened in the room, "Please stand if I call your name (she named the four students who were helping in the back). As I walked in today I noticed each of you going above and beyond to help Mr. Chrysler in the back of the room. This shows the kind of spirit we have here . . ."*

Her practice of looking for detail helped her physiology and improved the context of her speech.

To do: Prior to a speech, look for positive detail around you. You do not need to use the information in a speech, although you can; the practice is to get out of your head. By getting out of your head, your physiology will be more open and positive.

The more we are in our head prior to a presentation, the more physiologically awkward we can get. Watching for what you like around you can uptick your physiology and (bonus!) give you details to use in the talk.

**Start a presentation *in it* rather than *about it* in order to uptick physiology, especially when starting about it causes you discomfort, like it does Jason:**

*Jason's boss told him to make sure he introduced himself, thanked the audience, and gave an agenda.*

*However, each time Jason opened this way, it took him ten minutes to then get into his presentation. He kept getting feedback that he needed to work on his comfort in front of a room.*

*Jason realized that he was most comfortable when he was in it—showing off what the product could do. For his next presentation, he began with the story of a client using his system live—walking the audience through a moment with the product. After 60 seconds of wowing listeners with the product, he then introduced himself, thanked them for being there, and gave a quick agenda.*

Instead of trying to *get there* in a talk, try *starting there*. *Start* **in it.**

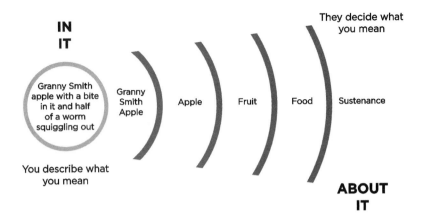

One of the challenges of public speaking is **using** your physiology rather than being **abused** by it. The practice mentioned above helps you relax your physiology a bit. The next practice helps you begin your presentation in a way that creates more physiological comfort.

I've coached many people in public speaking, and for most of them, starting in the middle of a story helps with both keeping physiology and nerves in check and getting the audience interested. You notice I didn't say **all** of them. Make sure you practice the idea here and make sure it works for you.

How will you know what works for you? What physiology should you aim for? Answer: The same physiology you experience when you're with your closest friends, on a good day, sober. In this state you're more real with your voice intonations, gestures, etc. We will dig more into this concept in the Storytelling portion of this chapter.

## Here is an example of how to begin a presentation *in it* with a story:

*Jill walks out on the stage and the lights blind her. She is nervous. Instead of telling the audience what she plans to talk about, she simply starts in the middle of a story. "My toes are one inch above the metal . . . I am hovering above railroad tracks vibrating from the force of an oncoming train. I can see the train conductor's face and blue hat as he stands at the horn. My brothers are holding my arms tightly from either side of the tracks as they laugh and tell me to 'say UNCLE!'"*

Most of the audience is listening to Jill intently because they have no idea where the story is going and want to know what happens next. They wonder what this story could have to do with surviving a bank audit, which is the topic of this presentation.

Jill is doing what she does all the time with her friends: starting in the middle of a story. She doesn't sit with her friends at a bar and say, "Today, we are going to talk about my day, then we are going to talk about your day, then we will order drinks." Nor does she tell them what she is going to say, then say it, then tell them why she said what she said. Instead, she starts in the middle of her story, then circles back to her main point.

Friends swap stories that are *relived* rather than manipulated to fit a certain goal. Because storytelling is central to relationship in our culture, we are in the habit of listening when we hear a story. Jill successfully uses this tactic in her presentation.

### Starting *in it* rather than *about it* improves physiology.

About eight seconds into the presentation, Jill's body stops performing. Since she isn't an actress, her physiology doesn't work really well in performance mode. Now that she is *reliving*, she is less aware of herself and more in the moment.

Thus, presenters who start **in it** to uptick their physiology also can increase listening in the audience.

### Opening a presentation in the middle of an example or story is a habit that can work for some.

A story is the transactional medium of relationships in our culture, exchanged between friends everywhere. Stories help people relate to one another—and this is true in a work context as well.

The goal in opening a speech with a story should not necessarily be to get the audience engaged. Why? It is really hard to get an entire audience to be engaged. In trying to force an audience into a particular mindset, the speaker is messing with natural physiology, which always will come across as awkward and can reduce influence. Rather, the goal in opening a speech should be to inhabit the relaxed physiology you'd have around close friends. To achieve this goal, starting *in it* rather than *about it*—in other words *reliving* a story rather than *retelling* it—is the way to go.

Starting with an example can also achieve the same goal, though remember: Not everyone likes examples, and your physiology may not be the kind that is comfortable telling them. Be flexible as you see what works for you and your audience.

### How a person *opens* a presentation helps with positive physiology.

What is the purpose of the opening of a speech? Many folks say it is to get the attention of the audience. This is a good goal, yet I believe the purpose of an opening is to get the speaker in a positive physiology. Do whatever you need to do to make sure you are open and not awkward. There are many types of openings to try, and we will dig into the ones that use this model.

We will walk through these examples using the model:

- Thanking the audience: Most of us do not do this well, and it causes us to stumble.
- Telling a joke: This works only if telling jokes makes us comfortable.
- Talking about what we are going to talk about: For most of us, this causes us to reduce positive physiology.
- Introducing ourselves: For many of us, this causes us to go into awkward physiology.
- In the middle of a story: This is the opening that tends to improve physiology for most speakers and most audiences.

### Thanking an audience.

Often in presentations a speaker will begin by thanking the audience. This is a nice gesture, yet if it is done in general it can cause weird physiology in the room. It can be more powerful when the speaker uses **context** to express gratitude and examples to make the "thank you" come alive.

## Here is an example of how to apply context to a *thank-you* opening:

*Hillary stands in front of a room of 250 women and says, "Thank you for having me."* Eh. Not so memorable and it causes her physiology to down-tick a little.

*Hillary stands in front of a room of 250 women and says, "Thank you for all you are doing to improve the world my granddaughter will grow up in."* This one is better. Has a bit of feeling and specifics in it.

*Hillary stands in front of a room of 250 women and says, "It took me 20 minutes to get to the front of this room—not because my pantsuit is too tight, but because each of you had photos to show me of the children you are helping in Malawi. Carol, I will always hold in my heart the story of Ubaon. I give all of you my deepest thanks for each hand you've held and for the work you're doing to positively change the world my granddaughter will grow up in."*

This is thanking a room so they *feel* thanked. Use thanking people to create a *feeling*—people remember how you make them *feel*. (And notice how Hillary combined "watching for what you like" and context to thank this room.)

Meetings and presentations are also a feeling. The goal of a meeting or a presentation is to engage the audience so they listen, remember and often become committed to some sort of action. Commitment is a feeling and thus meetings and presentations must optimize for the kinds of feelings that produce action.

**The purpose of thanking people is for them to *feel* something.** Context helps with that.

## Using context to tell a joke.

Have you ever listened to a speaker begin a talk with a joke that fell flat and didn't work? It may be because the speaker isn't particularly funny, the joke was inappropriate, the joke wasn't relevant to the topic, or it was told in a general way. You can use the Context Model to decide if the joke helps with the outcome you are trying to achieve:

- Does your physiology improve with jokes? If the answer is no, skip them.
- Does the joke make the audience feel small or cause you to seem like a jerk? If so, skip it.
- Does the joke have a detail you can bring up later?
- Specificity is the reason that some comedy is so funny.
- There's a tactic comedians often use in which they pick a specific detail from earlier in their set and "call it back" randomly later in their bit. Jerry Seinfeld executes this to great comedic effect.
- Next time you are with a group of friends, notice what was said right before everyone burst out laughing. You'll often find that a sentence or detail had been repeated from earlier in the conversation. This tactic can also be effective in a professional setting: Call back specific details from earlier in a presentation to make the latter part hold more interest.
- Does the joke add value? Use the Context Model to ensure there is some connective tissue between the joke and what you want folks to remember.

**Talking about what we are going to talk about.**

Folks often start with an agenda. Not a bad thing, yet it often starts the speech in a low-energy way. We can use the Context Model to open the speech with a more specific description of the **outcome** the audience will get from the agenda. One way to do this is to focus on **why** the audience cares and **what** it cares about.

---

### Here is an example that increases positive physiology and interest:

---

*"Raise your hand if you have ever had a customer scream at you because you had to deny the warranty?" Kelly opened her talk with the complaint she heard her team say most often. "Raise your hand if these calls are difficult for you. I am going to ask you a series of questions. Please listen very distinctly to the question because you should raise your hand only one time. Now, close your eyes. Raise your hand if you think these calls happen more than 50% of the time. 25? 15? 5? Thank you. Here is what I'm going to walk us through today (agenda is on the slide) with the outcome being to help us all with these calls."*

Instead of doing a dry reading of the agenda, Kelly lets them read it after getting very engaged. She did this by coming up with specific questions the audience members could find themselves in. Kelly can use the data collected in the question portion to teach the team how often these types of calls actually happen. (They happen only 5% of the time, yet 75% of the audience thinks they happen 50% of the time.)

If you must give the agenda, do it in a way that is interesting so your physiology doesn't get depleted and the audience members are interested (or can find themselves and what they want in the agenda).

**Introducing ourselves.**

Often speakers begin presentations by introducing themselves or reciting their bios. For a lot of speakers, their physiology gets a little flat in this practice. It may be better to have someone else introduce you, or introduce yourself later in the presentation.

When you do introduce yourself, think of two things in this book:

1.  What does the audience care most about? Pick the details that matter most to them.
2.  How can you deliver these in an interesting way?

---

### Here are three examples of introductions using the Context Model:

---

*"Hi. My name is Greta Smith and I am running for the school board because I believe it is our duty as a community to make sure every child graduates from high school: 26% of our kids are not graduating and we can improve this. As a pediatrician, I am most devastated when I see a young adult slip out of school and not reach their full potential . . ."*

In this example, by using specific detail, Greta uses the opening of her speech to focus on what the audience cares about. She used a statistic to support her decision to run and was able to include her bio as part of what the audience cares about.

*"Hi. My name is Fred Dodd and I have been a fire-fighter for 27 years. I can handle a five-alarm fire without breaking a sweat, yet filling out my son's college form makes me sweat buckets. I am here today to walk us through an idea . . ."*

Fred used the introduction to connect to what he was talking about.

*"Hi. My name is Winston Smith and I am here to help you see the story in your accounting data. Today I will walk you through a few items in your financials that may keep you from getting your IPO. In my past 35 years as a CPA, I have watched thousands of clients ring the bell on the NASDAQ, and my goal today is to see you do the same. There are three things . . ."*

Because Winston uses his introduction to make his talk about what the audience wants and not what *he* wants, he makes the audience members want to listen to him.

In an introduction, avoid reading your bio. Just give three pieces (at maximum) of detail.

Now that we have some practices that improve our physiology as the speaker using the Context Model, let's apply the theory to the audience.

**It is critical the presenter focus on what the audience cares about and how the listeners feel about themselves as they listen.**

**Get the audience to listen more.**

Using the Context Model, we can notice if the way we are presenting causes people to listen more and be curious about what we are saying or if it causes them to shut down. One way to make our physiology work for us is to use the Context Model at the "worm" level. The more specific we are, the more likely we will be **in it** rather than **about it**.

---

**Here is an example of how to use *context* in a presentation at work without triggering people into disinterest:**

---

*Food Level: I am going to tell you why we need to stop losing deals.*

- *By starting at a vague level first, we can reduce listening. Folks may get in their head and start disagreeing with you before you tell them why.*

*Fruit Level: We must look at our prices to stop losing deals.*

- *We are still putting the disagreement up front, which may cause folks to resist us.*

*Granny Smith Apple Level: We have an opportunity to increase profit by 23%.*

- *By beginning with specific opportunity, folks may be more interested in listening.*

*Worm Level: I was sitting in ABC client's office yesterday, negotiating terms on the deal. As I sat in that office with the plaid wallpaper—you know the one—I felt my stomach churning because our competition is offering deals I don't know how to match. We have lost 58% of our deals due to price. If you look up on this slide, you'll see the differentials on the deals we have lost. It got me thinking about ways we can streamline what we do to increase profit so we can get these deals. I met with each of you executives and discovered three ideas that could increase profits by 23%. I'd like to walk you through them now. My ask is that we dig into these ideas with specifics today and see if we can come up with the best solution.*

- *The room can find themselves in that room with the plaid wallpaper and their interest is piqued.*

The key to using **context** in an audience-focused presentation is to avoid putting an opinion or a broad sweeping statement up front, which will cause people to stop listening to understand and instead trigger them into listening to respond. If our first words tell the person they are wrong, they may begin defending their position while we try to explain our opinion. If they are listening to respond, they aren't listening. It is better to keep them curious as long as possible.

---

### Here is an example of how we can trigger an audience into response mode:

---

- *I am not sure we really know who our customer is. We are not good at execution.*
- *Not everyone in this room is held accountable.*

Opening a presentation with an accusation can cause listeners to become resistant. The goal of a presentation is to keep people listening longer.

Instead of starting with a broad sweeping statement that is at the Fruit Level (which can trigger people), start with something they care about or an example that gives them the feeling you want them to have.

**We can also open with an example at a specific level of context.**

---

### Here are examples of using specific context to direct attention:

---

*Jill says, "Our CEO set a plan for us to launch in China in 341 days. We have three decisions to make today to keep us on schedule for that target. I have seven slides to walk you through now to give you the context required for the conversation. Feel free to ask questions as we go through this information."*

*Or:*

*Jill says, "We sent the S1 to the FCC at 10 a.m. this morning. This means we have 30 days to receive their commentary, at which point we will drop everything we are doing to respond.*

*There will be four teams: Finance, Regulatory, Product, and Global. Susie, you cannot release any press about product that is larger than 4% of our revenue or the FCC will give us an amendment and cause us to lose our September 14 target date."*

**A good practice is to put yourself in the position of audience members and answer their question: "What's in it for me?"**

When I say "me" I do not mean me or you; I mean *them,* the people you want to influence. They care most about themselves and are almost always tuned into the radio station WIIFM (What's In It For Me).

People want to find themselves and what they care about in what you're saying. So to truly listen, they have to imagine that what you are saying applies to them specifically. Sooner instead of later help people find *themselves* in what you are saying.

In the example about launching in China, Jill started *in it* rather than *about it* because she let the listeners know exactly why they should care about what she was saying: Their CEO wanted something and Jill gave details as to how they could make it happen. Jill didn't say, "We need to launch soon"; she used a specific number of days. She spoke to the *why* of what she was asking for and did so at a specific level of context.

When developing your presentation, think about the **audience** members and what they **specifically** care about.

If you can find specific examples of what they care about, you will be more believable.

---

### Here is an example of using specific context to direct attention:

---

- *Everyone in this room wants more time off. (Fruit Level)*
- *We can bring back summer hours when we land on these two deliverables. (Granny Smith Level)*

- *August 1st at 12 p.m. we will all go home early and avoid rush hour if we can land on these two deliverables. (Worm Level)*

**When planning your speech, presentation, or pitch, make sure your orientation is toward the *specific* audience you are addressing and what it cares about.**
This will require some research and curiosity before you prepare your speech. Don't pander; be curious.

### *Storytelling: The content of your speech and your ability to make it interesting.*

Storytelling is one method to increase positive physiology and audience interest as well as create something the audience is more likely to remember. It's an effective communication tool when the model is applied to make the stories optimal.

Storytelling is the transactional medium of relationship in our culture. Storytelling (and using examples) works because it is a habit most folks do all the time in their personal lives. It is how the best brands sell themselves and what the most famous leaders use to inspire their employees and customers.

We engage in storytelling as a habit when we are with our closest friends, often launching right into a story before we even sit down.

---

### Here is an example of how we use storytelling as a habit without even realizing it:

---

*Kelly enters a bar to meet her friend Kim. Even before they finish hugging hello, Kelly begins telling Kim what happened to her on the way: "So I'm sitting on the bus, minding my own business, and this woman licks my hand!"*

Because storytelling is something we do with our closest friends, we automatically listen to a story even if the speaker is a stranger—by force of familiar habit. When someone tells a story at a specific level of context as if it is happening *right now*, we get lost in the possibility of it all.

## Warning: Storytelling is a feeling.

Storytelling is a beautiful art that is often done in a transactional way. I caution people on the practice of using a story in a way that is transactional—in other words, telling a story just to get something you want. There are a couple of ways to know if you are using this medium in a way that could actually reduce influence (and make you look like a manipulator):

1. If your story is too obvious. If you are telling a story of working hard to convince people to work hard or if the "moral" of the story is clear from the beginning, you'll reduce curiosity.

2. If you are telling a story with deep emotion and you aren't actually feeling that emotion. I believe people should avoid storytelling if they aren't going to *feel* it or *relive* it. We can use examples of other people as a tool, but storytelling has a deeper physiology and human connection.

## Storytelling isn't always done well in business situations.

I started teaching storytelling more than two decades ago. Storytelling—and starting in the middle of a story in a specific way—increases listening because people are in the habit of telling stories to one another. To be interesting, storytelling is best told in a **vivid** way with some level of the unknown.

If you are going to use the Context Model to tell a story, let's first talk about how **not** to do it.

## Storytelling is a beautiful thing humans use to connect.

It has been cheapened a bit by folks who use it in an obvious transactional way.

What do I mean by *transactional?* When we are obviously trying to manipulate. For example, avoid telling a story about working hard in an attempt to get people to work hard. Obvious examples—even when told in storytelling form—don't work as well as subtle examples do. If a parent says to their child, "I used to walk three miles to school every day in the snow . . . uphill," that story is intended to get the child to realize how lucky they are, yet it doesn't hit the target because it is so obviously transactional.

Storytelling is how we communicate with our dearest friends. When people know we are transacting or trying to buy their influence with cheap tricks, we reduce influence.

---

### Here is an example of a good story told in a way that feels too transactional to be effective:

---

*At a meeting Lauren, a CEO, told her team the riveting story of how she became an Olympic swimmer. She ended by asking her team to "go the extra mile" and take more risks. Although she got an obligatory applause, it was clear that something just hadn't landed.*

Maintain your listeners' curiosity by refraining from making obvious points. If your speech feels too transactional, it may not land.

## Telling stories of imperfection can be effective.

Often stories that show perseverance carry the most influence. When people in positions of authority are willing to admit their own imperfections, other good things often happen. When we tell only the stories of our own heroism, sometimes folks stop listening.

---

### Here is an example of how Lauren could have talked about perfection:

---

*The sun is glaring off the water and I can't see the crowd. I'm not sure if my dad is watching. I'm ready to perform my first dive at my first dive event. I suddenly wish I'd opted out of being on the team. What made me think standing in front of my school in a red swimsuit was a good idea? I could smell the exhaust from the equipment on the roof of the building. That smell and the Cheerios I had for breakfast weren't making friends in my stomach. My first dive required a run and jump, and all I could think about was the quarter-size scars on my brother's back. He had slipped on a diving board and came out of the water with two abrasions that caused him a lot of pain.*

*I botched my first dive. Why? I was crippled by the fear of botching it. I was well trained and ready—it was my head that failed me. I love how my coach handled it—by telling me what I did right. In doing that, she gave me something positive to focus on in my next dive. She helped me get out of my head and risk again.*

*The second dive? Botched again. Big time. I am convinced my need to be perfect drove me to fail. Sometimes, I act here like that kid on the diving board. The slightest imperfection and I get in my head. What that does is squash innovation and risk in this company. Here is a plan I have to increase innovation/risk/faster failure in our firm—please check it out. I'd love your input and edits. For us to win in 2016 we must innovate . . .*

(The team will likely ask, "What happened at the dive meet?" That is how storytelling usually works. It makes people curious.)

Personal storytelling isn't required at work. If you are going to use a personal story, make sure you are IN the feeling of the story when you tell it.

## Let's look at the model again. What is in it really?

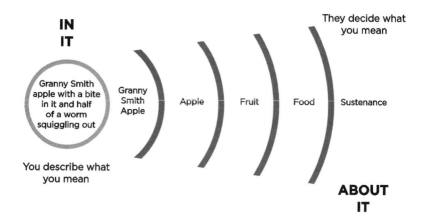

Often folks think they are **in** it when they are still **about** it.

- *I am going to tell you about a time I was embarrassed. (FOOD level)*
- *I was 17 years old. (FRUIT level)*
- *I often got picked up from school by my dad. (APPLE level)*
- *My dad picked me up from school. (Granny Smith level)*
- *I heard the screeching sound and smelled the smoke before I saw the car. My dad was driving his old 1973 Dodge Dart to pick me up from school. If you have ever heard the song, "My Hooptie," the car in that song is a Rolls Royce compared to this one. As the car wobbled up to the curb, I saw it out of the corner of my eye. (Worm level)*

**Start at the Worm Level.**

Starting at the Worm Level often engages the audience members as they get **in it** with you. The key here is to relive the story as if it were happening right now rather than to say "I remember . . ." or to talk about several moments. Pick one specific moment you can make come alive for 15 to 20 seconds. It should have color, detail, action, and sensory moments. Focus on starting in the middle of a story without giving away the point of the story. Leave the punch line unknown.

**Stories typically have some sort of drama in them, and *context* helps you narrate that drama.**

Here is a graphic of how a story can go.

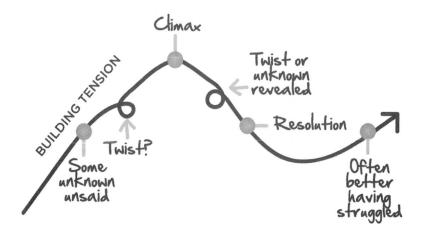

Use detail to build the anticipation in a story. It is better to describe the tension with detail rather than say "it was tense."

## An example of building tension:

The book wouldn't say "Ellen was scared." It would describe what was happening so the reader feels scared: Ellen felt a fine trickle of sweat slowly descend from her forehead as the alien's face came within a half-inch of hers.

**The same principle stands for building excitement. Use layers of context—specific examples and vivid, personal details if appropriate—to help build excitement in a story.**

This is the point when some folks get their socks in a twist because they assume personal stories are necessary to influence people. I once had someone in the audience shout, "I am *not* going to tell childhood stories of playing Beer Pong in my mother's prom dress!"

Sharing personal stories isn't a requirement. Any story told to an audience the same way it'd be told to a friend can increase listening, unless the listener in question loathes storytelling and responds only to buzzwords. In that case see Chapter Two on what makes your specific audience listen, and do more of that.

---

## Here is an example of how to build excitement using a story that is not personal:

---

*Marla and I are sitting on white leather couches in the fanciest reception area I have ever seen. The art on the walls belongs in the MoMA, the receptionist offered us seven different types of water, and I swear there was a live three-piece band instead of a radio. I was starting to get nervous. Then Marla jumped up and started talking with the receptionist; you know Marla is good at small talk. I heard Marla ask, "How do you sit in front of all these chocolates and not gorge on them all day?" The receptionist whispered to her, "The secret is I never fill that crystal bowl with my favorites." They laughed. Marla asked her what kind was her favorite. The conversation was interrupted by the CEO, who led us into a conference room the size of a football field. The meeting went okay, not great. I think my nerves got the best of me. I wasn't able to show him how special we are. This morning I received a phone call from the CEO. "We need you and Marla to pitch to our executive team; you are being considered." I was dumbfounded. I was almost going to say I was surprised when she interrupted my thoughts with this: "There is something special about your company. Our receptionist can't stop raving about what you did." I was hoping she'd tell me what because I had no idea. As it turns out, Marla mailed the receptionist her favorite chocolates with a note thanking her for her kindness that day. The CEO said, "Clearly, your team has some disruptive ideas on PR that we need to hear; can you be here tomorrow by 2 p.m.?"*

The story has twists, turns, and drama. He doesn't start the story with "I'd like to thank Marla for incredible ingenuity." Instead, he relives the moment as if it is happening *right now.* In storytelling, it is important to use details rather than buzzwords. If you are going to use storytelling, make the story interesting.

**Be fact-based instead of buzzword-based.**

Often we do use buzzwords in speeches to help people find themselves in what we are saying. If you're going to use a buzzword when storytelling, be sure to back it up with a specific example so everyone knows what you mean.

### Here is an example of converting a buzzword into an example:

*We need to increase velocity.*
vs.
*On April 1, Carol Smith will walk into her warehouse and gasp with delight when she sees that our product arrived to her on time and under budget.*

*We have two weeks to make this happen. Who has an idea?*

---

## Here is an example of the difference between an example and a superlative:

---

*The engineering team did a great job.*

*vs.*

*I walked into the office on a Sunday morning to the smell of pepperoni pizza. I heard a hum of voices and the clicks and clacks of keyboards. As I cocked my head to one side listening, I kept my phone in my hand, just in case we were being robbed. As I turned the corner, there were all our engineers, sitting in a giant mess of stuff—wildly working on something. What were they doing? A month ago they presented to the executive team a plan to reduce our outages that as a company we couldn't afford to have. So what did this team do? It created a HACKATHON from Friday night until Sunday morning. Unbelievable dedication! As my show of thanks . . .*

Saying *Great Job!* doesn't always make people feel great. Opening a presentation with *Great Job!* doesn't give the speaker or the audience the energy it could if it were more specific. Avoid beginning speeches with superlatives; use examples instead. Part of the reason this is important is to increase audience member engagement and what they remember. Again, the brain remembers what is most vivid.

## Help people remember and take action by using stories.

Remember the Cognitive Illusions from Chapter Six? How our brain isn't perfect at storing, retaining and interpreting information? With all of the stuff our brains take in, we often remember what is most vivid. The more detailed we are in our description, the more **in it** we become. The audience can then get lost in the moment during our presentation rather than be distracted by how uncomfortable their plastic chairs are.

If we provide vivid details we create mindshare with our listeners, and that increases the likelihood they will remember something we've said. The more specific a memory, the more it sticks with a person over time.

When we use details or examples in storytelling, we can help an audience remember what we've said.

---

### Here is an example of using a detailed story to help people remember something important:

---

*It is 1995 and there is a piece of furniture in every office called a file cabinet. I needed to teach someone our filing system and one specific safety measure: Don't pull two drawers out of the file cabinet at once.*

This statement is a bit forgettable; it is hard for us to find ourselves in that sentence and I didn't say it in a way that increases listening.

A more vivid (WORM level) way to express it:

*I am standing in the middle of an office with the ugliest green carpeting and yellow walls. I had dressed meticulously to look older than I was, wearing a skirt, heels, and Sheer Energy pantyhose. I was 19 years old and it was my first day working at a collection agency. I was filing in the cabinets in the middle of the collection floor, and I was shocked as I listened to collection agents insult and attack debtors over the phone.*

*All I wanted was to get out of the negativity of that room. I decided I could file more quickly if I kept the drawers open. Moments later,* **slam!***—the filing cabinet tipped over and I had to jump back to avoid being crushed. I almost cleared it until the corner of the filing cabinet snagged my skirt, pulling it down and exposing my gumball-machine underwear for all to see! So embarrassing!*

I've told that story to all the file clerks I've ever hired (back when there were filing cabinets), and they always remember it—I even got gumball machines as presents sometimes. They remember it both because specificity is memorable in our brains and because I tell it in a way that increases listening—starting **in it** ("I am standing in the middle of an office . . ."), not **about it** ("I'm going to tell you a story now . . .").

## With regard to editorializing in storytelling, less is more.

Using a story to teach works best when the action we want a person to take is simple, easy, and direct.

One way influencers reduce the effectiveness of storytelling is by making long-winded general requests. Conversely, influence is often increased when the action we want someone to take is an easy next step.

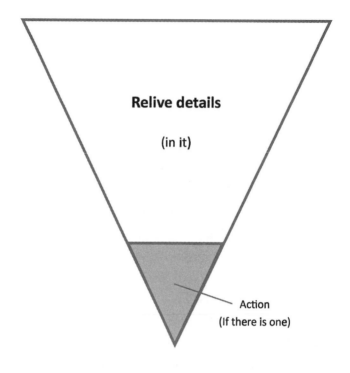

---

## Here is an example of using storytelling at work:

Ed tells a story about his paper route when he was a kid. He uses incredible detail and has the entire legislature (the folks who will vote on his bill) mesmerized. He then ends his story with a long-winded list of things the legislature must do for kids. He loses some of his influence by giving the audience so much to think about.

Instead, using the Context Model, Ed can get very specific about what he wants to happen. "AB 357 is in your committee; vote yes because your legacy is at stake. Be the legislator who lives up to the promise of youth."

## Here is another example of using this idea in sales:

Christy has an entire hospital board listening as she tells her story of reducing patient wait times by 41%. Her charts and graphs prove that the impact to the bottom line is astounding in both patient satisfaction and profit. At the end of her talk she asks for the order, for them to sign a contract. This is not an easy next step for the board. Board members disconnect and say they are not sure if they are ready. Instead, Christy can finish her presentation with a specific question: "What questions do you have?" or "As you think about your hospital, what questions are top of mind?" or "An easy next step, if you are interested, is to walk your nursing staff through . . ."

**Having a specific *ask* that is easy to do will increase influence. Make it easy for the audience to say yes.**
What I mean is, when storytelling:
- Give more detail and less editorializing and telling people what your story means; spend more time being *in it* and experiential. (If you feel the need to explicitly state your story's meaning, keep it to a one-liner.)
- Do *less* scripting or writing out of the story.
- Tell *fewer* stories that detract from your focus.

Instead:
- Use *more* details that are relevant to the story and that people can identify with personally.
- Use very specific pieces of detail even if they seem bizarre or out of place; these really allow people to visualize what you're describing. For example: "The three-of-hearts card was pinned to my bike's axle, and

it made a clacking sound as I pedaled down Shady Oak Drive."

- *Relive* your story instead of *reciting* it.

**Details are seeds.**

You do not have to use a lot of words of detail. One reason for detail is to help the audience find THEMSELVES in the story. If I describe breakfast cereal, it doesn't help you find yourself in my comment. Yet if I plant a seed of recognition by specifically citing *Raisin Bran*, folks in the audience remember when they had Raisin Bran as a kid. This does two things: they are now IN the talk with us and there is mindshare. They are more likely to remember what we talked about the next time they see that cereal.

The latter is the least important. The former is what really creates relationships with listeners. Give three words of specific REAL detail, not some gross made-up thing to pander to the audience. The more random the detail, the more specific, the more likely it will connect.

Examples of details that help people find themselves in your story:

- Pet OR My dad's pet tarantula named Fuzz
- Shoes OR Penny Loafers, yes, with a penny in the slot
- Sweatpants OR Lululemon Yoga Pants, the opaque version
- Coffee OR a Grande Latte Low Foam No Sweetener
- Rollerskates OR Black and White Low-Ride Speedskates with Riedell Wheels
- Favorite song OR *Rapper's Delight*, the longer version

Even if the person doesn't know the song, their automatic response is to connect to a detail in their lives.

I can't say this enough, do not plan this stuff to match what you think the audience will have in their memory. RELIVE the story and find YOUR details—those work best in planting seeds.

**Help your audience remember with epigrams.**

After audience members leave, we want them to remember what we said. One way to improve the effectiveness of presentations is to use the Context Model to create epigrams and one-liners.

Short, catchy phrases stick with people. These phrases are often at a more specific level of context, which is why they are so repeatable. Some examples include:

- Leaders get the organization they deserve. (Rand Stagen)
- A complaint means a person stands for something. (Robert Kegan)
- How people feel about themselves dictates commitment vs. compliance. (me)
- The team member beside you is as important as the customer in front of you. (me)
- The number one goal of a debt collection call is to establish enough relationship so the person tells you the truth. (me)

Epigrams help people repeat and remember what we talked about.

**Use the context tool to recognize the specific things you do that create influential presentations.**

*Make sure you have a system or*
*process to improve presentations.*

Notice the stuff you do that audiences seem to like. Identify specific phrases that audiences react to and re-use them while speaking. (It's helpful to write these phrases and keep them with you.)

Read the sentence in the parentheses again. Write down the stuff you say to an audience that you notice works for it. If you say something and it sticks, use it again. Often we go through a list of what we did wrong and forget the stuff we did that really worked for us. Notice when the audience responds and write down what worked.

Rather than write a speech, live a speech. Keep a journal of the details in stories you love that happen around you. Then, when it comes time to prepare for a speech, you can flip through these examples and see if one of them fits.

## A Deliberate Practice

Keep a journal of interesting stories; practice telling them—being *in it*—with your friends and family and see how they respond. The more interested you are in a subject, the more interested the audience will feel.

## Can I keep a journal of examples and stories with lots of specific details I find interesting to use in future presentations?

# Chapter Ten

# Feedback

Feedback is one area of communication that often leads to reduced listening and understanding. Does it seem more difficult to get a positive behavioral response when giving people feedback? Often that's because we aren't skilled at giving feedback in a way that matches its purpose. Feedback is not supposed to be a monologue with one person talking and the other person listening. Feedback that sways to create a change in behavior is a dialogue.

Remember: How we do anything is how we do everything, which is why this book is about a model you can apply to **all** communication. If we focus only on "presentation-speak," then when it is time to present, we will have to **try** to use a tool. If we practice types of influence that work in presentations all the time—even during feedback—we are more likely to present well because of good habits rather than performance.

## Feedback is a conversation meant to improve outcomes.

We often provide feedback in a way that doesn't lead to the desired outcome. Feedback must be specific and attached to something people care about for it to be meaningful and lead to action. When people can identify themselves and their concerns in feedback, they are moved to understand it and *want* to do something with it.

Feedback should:

- Feel like it is being said *for* the recipient rather than *at* the recipient.
- Be offered to direct reports, peers, and others in a way they will be open to hearing and receiving it.
- Move you and the recipient closer to the outcome you want.
- Create a culture of feedback—an environment in which people are always improving.
- Help people improve their abilities by treating them as individuals.
- Be actionable and specific.

### The best feedback is as specific and fact-based as possible.

Use the levels of context to test the specificity of your feedback. Generalized feedback can cause defensiveness, confusion and misplacement of focus on the part of the listener.

Check out the Context Models below with varying levels of context for the feedback **communication**. **Communication** is much too vague for a person to know what they need to work on. **Communication** could mean "update me more often."

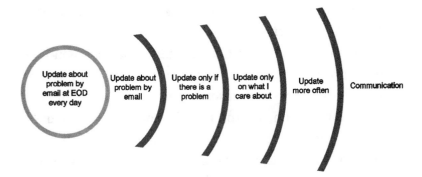

The feedback **communication** could also mean, **speak up in meetings** instead of **update me more often** as above. Using the Levels of Context model below, notice how the feedback **communication** meant as **speak up more often** can still be fairly vague. The more specific we are the more likely a person can convert the feedback into behavior.

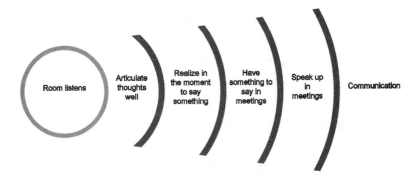

If what we meant by communication was to email less, we did not accurately convey our point with the above version of **communication**. Without an example or specifics, generalized feedback is nonexistent or distracting feedback.

**Feedback in the form of a broad, sweeping statement can feel like an attack.**

If feedback is too general, it has little value and often feels like an attack or criticism. In other words, it will aim to sway but will most likely shove instead! Most of us want to improve our communication, yet the meaning of that term is quite vague. If you tell me that I need to improve my communication, what action can I take? Perhaps I'll think, "Okay, I'm going to talk more in meetings," when what you really want is for me to be more concise in meetings. General feedback does not lead to the desired results.

"You need to work on your communication" can feel like an admonishment. You are telling me that something is wrong with me and in a way that I can't really address it.

If you said to me, "Yesterday, you told me after the product meeting that Joe has the specs wrong. I missed that and I am thankful for the catch. Did you notice the error during the meeting?" If I say yes, you know to coach me to speak up in the meeting. If I say no, the feedback I need to give about speaking up isn't relevant.

**Examples help us give relevant feedback.**

*Use fact-based examples in feedback;*
*don't tell people what they mean or how they feel.*

Use the levels of context to test whether your feedback is specific and fact based or meaning based.

| | |
|---|---|
| *"Work on communication."* | ← Joe has no idea what to change. He may start talking more, when what you want him to do is listen more and talk less. |
| *"You talk a lot because you lack confidence."* | ← This is more specific, yet now Joe is in his head, resisting the meaning you're trying to force on him. |
| *"You won't let anyone get a word in edgewise in sales meetings."* | ← A little more specific, yet the "example" you've given is too general. When did he do it, and with whom? |
| *"Your lack of confidence in yesterday's meeting with Susie was apparent to everyone."* | ← Again, this is somewhat more specific, yet it doesn't explain what Joe did in a fact-based way. A comment on Joe's confidence will not be helpful here. |
| You: *"Joe, what do you think about what Susie said during yesterday's meeting about shifting our platform to handheld?*<br><br>Joe: *"I wasn't listening."*<br><br>You: *"You have to know what Susie said in order to influence what happens next Why were you talking over her?"*<br><br>Joe: *"Because I think Susie is stupid and dimwitted. She should not be on the team!"* | ← Now that you've addressed Joe's specific behavior, you can address the real issue that's exposed. The more specific and fact-based your comments, the more likely it is they will lead to a productive conversation. |

Notice how much easier it becomes to talk about Joe's behavior when we get more specific. We now can have a productive conversation about it—and may even solve some conflict in the process! The more specific I am, the more likely I am to tell Joe something he can act on.

## Avoid labeling behavior when offering feedback.

A common mistake while giving feedback is labeling behavior in a nonspecific way. For example:

| | |
|---|---|
| *"You are losing credibility."* | ← This doesn't help anyone improve; it only makes them feel attacked. |
| *"You lost credibility in the meeting yesterday."* | ← This is more specific, yet it still uses a label, which will trigger undesirable behavior. |
| *"Did you notice the CEO push away from the table and cut us off in that meeting yesterday? He did that right after you interrupted him three times. I'm thinking he doesn't like being interrupted. What do you think?"* | ← This feedback is fact-based, curious, and doesn't directly label the person's behavior as problematic. Specific = good. |

Can you see how the more specific my feedback, the more likely the recipient is to take action addressing the behavior? In contrast, can you see how attacking credibility will only ensure the recipient stays in his head, unable to enact the desired change?

## Be curious and ask questions that drive toward specifics.

In the last three examples, I demonstrated feedback as a curious ask rather than as a one-way conversation. That's because I believe feedback should be more of a question than a statement, a dialogue, not a monologue.

Sometimes our questions may accidentally generate a yes/no response or a one-word answer, but avoid that if possible; it's usually better to ask questions that'll get a person talking. For example:

> *What are three things you noticed in the meeting yesterday?*

Notice how I didn't ask the person to *grade* the meeting. Avoid asking questions that cause a person to give a number or letter rating because these responses are too vague to be useful. Ask questions that get examples at the worm level. An example of a question *not* to ask:

> *How was the meeting yesterday?*

This question invites a one-word answer, like "Good," and where can you go from there? Instead, ask questions that provoke specifics. (I hope you see how this is using the Context Model levels to gather more data.) For example:

> *What did you notice in the ABC company meeting?*

The feedback you give will depend on the way in which this question is answered. In other words, you will tailor your feedback to the response you get. Some potential responses:

1.  *"I suck at this. I don't think I'm good at sales."*
2.  *"They're the wrong client for us. They only care about price, and we can't meet it."*
3.  *"There was a moment when I lost the deal. Can you coach me on what I could have done better?"*
4.  *"I rocked it. I'm sure they're going to sign."*

Let's imagine that the feedback you want to give is that the client's three questions during the meeting went unanswered. In Scenario 1—"I don't think I'm good at sales"—you'd dig deeper to figure out what is going on with your coachee's confidence. In Scenario 2—"They're the wrong client for us"—you'll want to find out more about why the coachee feels this way before you start coaching. In Scenario 3—"Can you coach me?"—you have a clear opening. In Scenario 4—"I rocked it"— you have the opportunity to ask questions to find out what she is thinking.

Ask questions that will help you get inside the head of the person to whom you are giving feedback. Don't ask questions with the sole purpose of getting this person to share your sentiments. Tricking people into agreeing with you through the use of manipulative questions is not cool. Here is an example of questions that feel manipulative:

*Joe wants Susie to agree with the elimination of color choices from a new product, so he asks her a series of leading questions that paint her into a corner. By the time he officially asks her to get on board with the decision, she has no choice but to agree. Not cool. Even if she nods in his presence in part because she feels manipulated, it will create backlash after she's left the room.*

**Sometimes your facts will not align.**

If your perception of the facts does not align with another person's, consider it an opportunity to begin a dialogue and a chance to learn more about the person as well as to examine your own biases. Instead of trying to be *right*, be curious. You may be mistaken about what you think you saw, and by asking the right questions you're more likely to discover that you took a trip down misperception highway.

A big part of making feedback stick is convincing the recipient to see you as an ally who's trying to help him move toward something positive for *both of your sakes*.

Note: If you are the kind of leader who brightens a room by leaving it, you may never get someone to align with you on the facts. If people are protective of themselves around you— if they get defensive even when you're just saying hello—you likely don't get a lot of commitment from them (at best, you probably only get compliance).

**Give feedback that will prompt one small, easily applied action.**

People often give feedback on an action that is too big. We often ask people to change too many behaviors at once. In feedback, use the Context Model to identify the "micro-behaviors" that need to change for a given resulting behavior.

Let's use the example of "You need to speak up in meetings." This *sounds* good; it is a clear action. Yet if you really think about it, "speak up in meetings" is still rather broad— and it also may feel a bit like an accusation. When we explain long division to kids, we don't begin by giving them a pencil and telling them to figure out how many times 37 goes into 532. We teach them the smaller parts first. The same goes for the feedback we give our team.

So, what do you have to be good at to speak up in a meeting?

First, let's think of the behaviors a person needs to be good at to speak up in a meeting:

- Managing conflict
- Thinking of an opinion in the moment
- Articulating their opinion quickly
- Listening to what others are saying
- Pushing back
- Having confidence in their opinion

See the example in the ***context*** model below. It is populated with the "Resulting" behavior of "speak up in meetings." The resulting behavior is a concatenation of many behaviors. If a person doesn't know ***how*** to change their behavior, they will not change it.

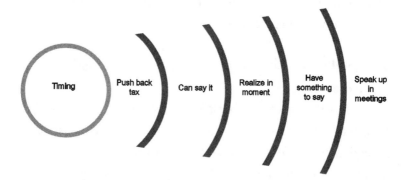

Can you see how different your feedback would be for someone if you knew ***which*** layer of "speak up in meetings" was their trouble area? If we put this in the model, we can see how "speak up in meetings" is too vague to convert the feedback into a new behavior. The model helps us see the microbehaviors about which we can provide feedback.

Let's try this again with another common feedback comment "Leadership Acumen."

Let's imagine that a manager tells a team member, "You need to develop more leadership acumen." Telling someone to "develop leadership acumen" and expecting them to know what that means is like telling a pilot to pick up their waiting passengers "in the United States." Where in the United States? Which airport? Which gate?

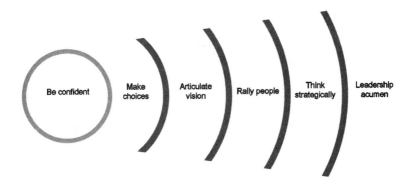

Be confident — Make choices — Articulate vision — Rally people — Think strategically — Leadership acumen

Feedback requires just as much specificity. "Leadership acumen" is too vague a term for a person to understand or execute. Even if you've just given the person specific feedback full of fact-based examples, if you end your conversation by requesting a super-broad behavior you'd like them to develop, they'll either be lost or focused on something you hadn't intended.

### Combine asking with "feedbacking."

To give specific feedback we should know the specifics of the situation, so talk to the person in question and ask him what he is thinking; he will likely have something to say. Talk to her about how her contribution to meetings is critical—how it both serves her career and is in the best inter-ests of the organization. Coach him on how to do it, and if he doesn't, ask why not.

---

### Here is an example of feedback as a conversation:

---

- *What are you thinking about the meeting?*
  - *The deadline is impossible.*
- *Why?*
  - *Three of the team members go on mater-nity leave in April.*
- *Oh. Why didn't you mention that?*
  - *I assumed people knew.*
- *One of the things I hear you talk about is how we often don't stick to deadlines. This frustrates you, correct?*
  - *Yes, very.*
- *If you keep quiet in meetings, that will continue. If you want to change it, give the details!*
  - *Well, I don't like conflict.*
- *Exactly. You're going to have conflict when your team doesn't hit the deadline, right? So, either speak up now, or deal with conflict later.*
  - *If I say the deadline is impossible, people will yell.*
- *Not if you offer multiple options. For example, "We have three women going on maternity leave in April. Our options are 1) Keep the deadline and hire outside expertise. 2) Push the date to September. 3) Adjust the scope of the project."*

- *Hmm. . . Okay, let me try that.*
- *Good, let's do it. I'll call everyone back inside.*

In this example, the leader gets curious and uses the model to get to specifics of **why** the person isn't doing the behavior the leader wants to give feedback on. Perhaps it isn't feedback the person needs at all. It is coaching.

## Catch people *in* the example—give feedback in real time.

We can use the Context Model levels in real-time coaching moments. Levels of context can be used with respect to timing. Because memory changes reality in our head—and most of us believe everything we think—feedback should be relayed sooner rather than later, so time has no opportunity to distort what happened.

We can give feedback during different times:

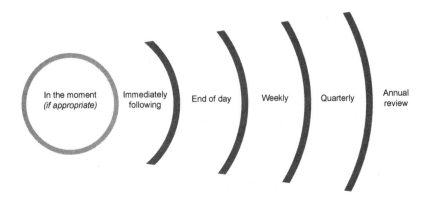

The longer you wait to give feedback, the less likely recipients still will find themselves in the situation you are referencing. Feedback closer to the event carries more weight.

The more **in the moment** we give feedback, the more likely there will be enough detail to apply the feedback. And often the best way to accelerate the behavioral result in feedback is to catch people **doing** what it is we want them to do in the moment.

### Spotlight the specific behavior you want to see when people exhibit it.

We talked about thanking people in the presentations portion of this book and how effective it can be using specifics. Being appreciative of a strength during feedback follows the same thinking. When we are specific, we actually accelerate the behavior we are looking for.

---
### An example of catching someone in the new behavior:
---

*John asked Susie to speak up in meetings. Specifically, he told Susie to push back when she doesn't think something is possible. In a following meeting, Susie asks a clarifying question for the first time ever, and the CEO is forced to describe in more detail what the end result will be and how to prioritize to make it happen. Asking for this explanation is a huge leap forward for Susie.*

*John stops Susie directly after the meeting and says, "I don't know what would have happened had you not asked that clarifying question. Did you see how many other people in the room were unclear on the deadline? More of that, Susie. Your speaking up saved us a lot of time."*

**Be descriptive. (Don't just use a superlative.)**

### *Spotlight the specific behavior you want to see.*

Avoid doling out general superlatives and grades; instead, give specific feedback. For example, if John had simply said, "Great job, Susie," it may have made her feel good but it wouldn't have touched her on a visceral, lasting level. Superlatives work for dogs, not for people. Besides, "great job" doesn't tell her specifically what it is she's done correctly.

---

### Here is an example of specific feedback that increases good feelings:

---

After Jose's presentation, you tell him, "Hey, Jose, great job on the presentation." Jose walks away thinking, *Awesome—he loved my PowerPoint.* You walk away thinking, *Jose did do a great job answering people's questions, but I've got to get him to stop creating 82-page PowerPoint presentations!*

Superlatives should always be backed up with specifics.

---

### An example of a specific positive feedback:

---

*Hey, Joe, your ability to take a tough moment in a sales meeting and turn it into an easy next step is just magical. Bravo.*

**In general, avoid giving any feedback that includes a superlative.**

When you notice that you are using a superlative, use a specific detail instead.

---

## Here is an example of directing behavior with positive feedback:

---

*If you say, "Great job, Susie," she has no idea what was great, what to repeat, if you are actually sincere, or if you just read a book about motivating your employees. This means that Susie will decide for herself what she found great about what she did—and it likely isn't the same thing you thought was great.*

*Similarly, if the head of product says to a team member, "You lost all credibility in that meeting," it is general labeling that often leads to misunderstanding. Alternatively, "Did you notice that the COO was shaking her head while you discussed the pricing and you never called on her?" would have been the way to produce results.*

**Practice communicating without superlatives all the time so it becomes easy for you.**

Here is an easy, deliberate practice for speaking less abstractly and without superlatives: From now on, when you are asked about a movie you just saw or a restaurant you recently visited, never answer with superlatives—*It was good* or *I hated it*. Instead, go to a more specific level of context with your answer. For example, *I loved it because of the weird menu, like the chocolate-dipped sea bass, and because all the servers acted like philosophers.*

## A positive plus a negative = zero.

So far we have talked about how to give feedback that adjusts behavior and spotlights positive behavior. Be careful you aren't reducing listening when you do both at the same time. In math class, most of us learned that + (positive) plus − (negative) = 0. When we preface negative feedback with a positive, we may cause the person not to listen to the positive at all. The purpose of positive feedback is to make a person feel appreciated, yet because of a worn-out formula of putting the positive feedback first, folks often do not hear the positive as they are bracing themselves for the negative. They will listen anticipating the bad rather than feeling the good.

Trouble is, even with a positive preface, most people still know the bad stuff is coming, which often means they won't hear the good stuff that came beforehand anyway.

I believe that specific positive feedback should not only stand alone but also should be given frequently. If you invest a lot in a person up front, when the time comes to correct something, you can just *say it* rather than beat around the bush. For example:

> *Hey, Joe, did you notice the client checked out at*
> *slide 38? I think we should cut the slides down to 15.*
> *Do you agree?*

"Wait," you say, "just giving the negative feedback feels so . . . negative!"

I guess that's true. Okay, if you simply *must* say something else here, make sure you *end* with the positive rather than beginning with it. For example:

> *Joe, cut the slides to 12. Agreed? Oh, and I am*
> *floored by your depth of understanding of the*
> *client.*

*Bravo! How'd you know about their three-day shipping lag?*

## Avoid "thamming" people.

What is "thamming"? It's "Thank you" spamming. We live in an age of email; thus our model and thoughts about feedback can also be applied to email.

The purpose of a thank-you email is to make sure people feel appreciated. There's a difference between saying thank you and actually meaning it.

- Spam: A generalized volume of information—a scattering of data you hope lands somewhere and means something to someone.
- Appreciation: A deliberate act meant to show recipients you are grateful for them and what they did.

Use levels of context when thanking someone. Sending an email to 20 people that reads, "Great job, thanks" is nice, but it doesn't create the special **feeling** that comes from specifics. If you say, "Great job, Susie! Thank you," Susie experiences about two seconds of appreciation, then moves on with her day. If you can evoke real feeling by your appreciation, the effect will last much longer. Here is an example of thanking someone that still uses a superlative, but is much more specific:

*Susie, there was a moment in the sales presentation when I was **certain** we'd lost the clients. They were hostile and complaining about price. Everyone in that room had a look of defeat. But then you leapt up, drew that model on the dry erase board, asked the client a series of questions, and at the end of the meeting they were right there with us. That* *wouldn't have happened without you, Susie, and I'm deliriously proud of how you take risks with sales prospects. You're a rockstar!*

If you say this to Susie, you may get an emotional hug, or even tears. If you email it to her, she likely will print it out, show her family, and keep it tucked away for the tough days.

If you are going to thank her, don't "tham" her—make her *feel* your appreciation by using the Context Model.

### Give examples for every buzzword.

When giving feedback, be selective in how you back up the use of buzzwords. Buzzwords are everywhere, which means that we often have to use them in conversation. This is okay— as long as you use examples to make sure your audience understands exactly what the buzzwords mean. Here are two examples of using both a buzzword and a specific example:

*Jack, you were incredibly nimble in the meeting yesterday. We spent days preparing that deck and presentation. When the CEO wouldn't let you show it, you just sat next to her and drew the options on her writing pad on the fly. Your ability not to get triggered by adjusting to the change in plan helped us get the budget we needed. Congrats, man.*

*Or:*

*June, next time you present to the CEO, make sure you have a backup plan so you can stay nimble. I noticed that when the CEO wouldn't let you show the deck, you just said okay and let your important issue drop off the agenda. How about we strategize on some ideas for the future?*

Play with context in your feedback. Remember, what's most important is how recipients feel about themselves while listening to you. Don't ever make them feel small or they can lose confidence, resist, or get complacent. Keep them open by creating a dialogue around specific facts and next steps.

## I am not an expert in parenting, yet so much of parenting is feedback.

So much of being a parent is communicating feedback to help kids live healthy lives. As we've shown, using examples is a great way to teach most things, but for children specifically, we can do one better. With children, use storytelling to convey important lessons that don't necessarily feel like lessons.

An additional way to use the Context Model for parenting is to ask questions to find out *why* the kids are doing what they're doing. If you can find out the why, you're more likely to get to the crux of the issue rather than wasting time addressing its symptoms.

---

### Here is an example of a parent who uses noticing specifics to improve outcomes:

---

*Maude screams as a Lego piece jabs into her bare foot. As she marvels at the incredible pain a silly plastic toy can administer, she feels rage toward her son who refuses to clean up his toys. She's tried everything. As he comes up the stairs, she is about to walk down that well-worn path that creates a compliant attitude from her son rather than a commitment from him for the future.*

*As her son turns the corner, she notices something.*

*She kneels next to the toys and asks her son what he is building. He gets very animated and tells her that after watching* Back to the Future, *he has decided to invent a hovercraft skateboard. He noticed that two magnets repel when placed next to each other, and he thinks he can use this energy to hover. "I haven't figured it out yet, Mom," he admits with a twinkle in his eye. She realizes that part of her anger came from the fact that she uses her home's cleanliness like a scorecard: clean house = good parenting. It hits her: This pile isn't a mess. It is her son's attempt at flight! That night, Mom and son make safety cones to put around experiments that should not be moved. As she moves him to different piles, he says, "Oh, that is a mess—sorry, Mom" and puts them away. As he learns the difference over time, the piles get less and less.*

Feedback doesn't always have to be a detailed soliloquy; it can be a series of questions that lead us to a new understanding of how to reach people.

## A quick to-do list about feedback:
- Use the Context Model.
- Give specific example-based feedback.
- Break down a new behavior into microbehaviors.
- Spotlight the behavior you want to see (be specific and frequent in your praise).
- Use context to become curious, and ask questions for deeper understanding.
- Focus on actions and specifics.

Avoid:
- Broad sweeping statements
- Broad behaviors
- Telling someone rather than asking

The next time you're giving feedback, avoid superlatives and use specific examples.

## Can I practice asking questions or giving feedback with specific actionable examples?

# Chapter Eleven

# Delegation and Direction

**Communication is a challenge when we are moving quickly and have many tasks in front of us.**

We often reduce understanding by transacting in ambiguity. If you use Context Model levels when making requests and setting direction, however, you'll improve your chances of effective results.

**Clarify and verbalize deadlines.**

If you are giving someone a direction, include the specific context of *when* you want your request completed. Don't say, "Please call the client and ask what size order she wants"; be precise about what you're asking for.

---

### Here is an example of using Context Model levels when giving directions:

---

*Please call ABC Company before noon and confirm that the order size is 175 tons. The order is on hold until we hear back from you—and it impacts our quarterly numbers. I need a response by 4 p.m. for the order to count.*

Yes, it takes a little extra time to include context, but those extra seconds will help people prioritize—and make sure you get what you want.

### Include specifics in the first email.

Even within my company, Allegory, where we teach this stuff, there are times we get vague with one another and end up having to exchange three emails instead of one.

---

### Here is an example of using levels of context when sending emails:

---

*If you say, "Review the Context book by Friday," what are you asking? What does* review *really mean? Does the person know specifically what to do?*

*Instead, say something like, "By Friday at 5 p.m., review and grammar-check Context book. Document on share drive under 'Projects.' Use Track Changes. If anything is unclear or needs more explaining, use Comments and highlight."*

*If this is a common action, create a word that means all of the above:*

- *Grammar (means do not question content; just make sure grammar is right)*
- *Content (Means grammar and content)*
- *Examples (means grammar, content, and add some examples)*

*We can shortcut the use of words in* Context *by having agreements up front.*

If you care about specifics, you have to mention them.

## Here is an example of using levels of context to improve outcomes:

*Don't tell your assistant to "pick up some wine," when what you truly want is white wine from the Russian River area that's not a screw cap and that's worthy of your biggest client. So instead of "Pick up some wine," why not say, "Pick up some white wine, $60–$120 price range, Russian River preferred. This is for my biggest client, and she is a wine aficionado."*

**Communicate the outcome desired.**

Use context or examples so it's crystal clear for the people you are delegating:

- What the end result should look like
- When you want it done
- What the budget is
- How to use or inform you
- What kind of decision-making power they have (e.g., when to include you)
- Limits to how much they can change the scope

## Here is an example of using specifics to improve outcomes:

If you say, "Mary, please handle," chances are that Mary will handle whatever it is in her own good time and however she wants. And sometimes that's a good idea. Other times it can be the kiss of death for your project. If you need Mary to do things in a particular way, you need to let her know that. For example:

*Mary, you are now in charge of the Gilligan Initiative. Here are the details:*

- *All seven people need to be off the island by Tuesday at 8 a.m.*
- *You can use only the resources we already have. There is zero budget.*
- *If you get any pushback/delays from the Professor, use me as needed.*
- *I do not need to be informed unless it will be delayed or isn't going to happen.*
- *You have full decision-making authority here.*

Using this Context Model may take longer, but it will often save hours in the long run.

**Giving directions.**

When giving directions, notice your level of context. Maybe you *want* to be vague so the person getting directions will own 100% of the outcome—and if that's the case, great. However, if you have specific preferences about how a job is to be done, you must voice them.

---

## Here are examples of using specifics to move people to action:

---

*"Figure out how to do this faster." (This is a high level of context, and that may be by design. Cool.)*
*Or:*
*"Can you figure out a way to reduce the ship date by four days?"*

*Or:*

*"We want to ship faster. Come up with some ideas and let me know what* faster *means to you.* (They will tell you what their goal is.)

### *Listen* for levels of context when receiving directions.

If someone says he needs something quickly, confirm what *quickly* means. *You* may decide it means three days from now; what *he* means is "in less than three hours."

You can create understood abbreviations for **when** in context:

- **Now** (drop everything)
- **EOD** (End of day)
- **EOW** (End of Week)

When giving directions, you can use examples, storytelling, and even imagery as well:

Practice painting a picture of what the end result will be so the persons taking on the project know what they are aiming for. We shouldn't micromanage on unimportant details and how precisely to do every part of a project. The key to using **context** for delegation is to reduce lack of clarity on the stuff that is truly important.

### Assign responsibility to an individual, not to a department.

Using the Context Model, make sure you are delegating a specific outcome to a specific individual.

---

## Here is an example of delegating in a large meeting:

---

*Lola needs engineering and product to work together to land on a page that wows the customer.*

*She paints a beautiful and vivid picture of the end result she desires and then tells all in the room they are responsible. By making everyone responsible, no one is responsible. Instead, using **Context** she says to the room, "Kelly and Kate, you two are the leaders of the outcome jointly. My expectation is your work together will result in these outcomes. What do you need from me to be successful?"*

If Lola doesn't make an individual responsible, accountability will falter.

## Invest time in improving outcomes rather than quicker conversations.

Taking a little extra time to explain in delegation and direction will increase how likely the end results will match your expectations.

**A Bonus Deliberate Practice**

Open phone calls and meetings with one question that gives you context:

"What do you want to make sure we get out of this phone call (meeting)?"

This one question can drive a conversation more toward real communication because it asks what matters most to the parties involved. See the below examples and notice how a conversation can have more clarity with varying answers to that question:

*Joann is a salesperson speaking with Garrett, a*

*prospect, for the first time. Imagine how different the call would be with each of these responses to the above question:*

- *I'd like to hear if you can come pitch to our executive team on Friday.*
- *I'd like to hear about your volume pricing models.*
- *I'd like to know why I should switch from a vendor I have been with for years.*
- *I'd like to hear your process for the xyz product and how quickly you can ship if we ordered by the end of the month.*

*Once Joann knows what Garrett wants, she can follow-up with questions so she can get clearer on the facts that help her solve the prospect's needs. If she talks about the value proposition of her business instead of Garrett's true specific wants, she is wasting valuable prospect interest.*

*Christina is taking her son Sebastian to Disneyland. He yells from the backseat of the car, "THE HAPPIEST PLACE ON EARTH, MOM!!!" Christina loves her sweet boy and wants him to have a glorious day. At breakfast she tells him a story (at a very specific level of context) about It's A Small World. "Honey, there will be really long lines, crowds and it will be hot out, yet there are moments at Disneyland you can't find anywhere else. When you are in line, you have to find a way to have fun while you wait for the fun. Let's talk about how we can make the lines fun . . . what are your ideas?"*

*Before they leave their pancakes and syrup, she*

*asks her six-year-old, "What do you want to make sure happens at Disneyland honey? What matters most to you?" Sebastian sweetly smiles, "MOM, I hear Tinkerbell flies across the sky. I just have to see that. Oh, and I want to go find the talking manhole cover." Mom realizes if she hadn't asked him that question, he would have missed what he was most looking forward to.*

Asking for examples and specific context at the beginning of phone calls, meetings and amusement park visits can improve the communication and experience.

## A Deliberate Practice

Notice how often instructions are vague and ambiguous. Use the Context Model in meetings to make sure the stuff that must be specific is verbalized.

## How specific are my instructions, and is it clear who is specifically accountable?

# Chapter Twelve

# Improving Conflict with Context

One of the challenges with conflict is that we often say silly, unproductive things when we are reacting, which distances us from the outcome we want. If we use levels of context in conflict to keep things *conversational* as long as possible rather than *confrontational*, we can move closer to the outcome we want.

**First, our operating system must be open rather than reactive. How do we do it?**

*Expect people to say things that trigger you.*

People often use triggering language when they are upset. Try not to get all hot and bothered about every word. Here is an example that often happens in conflict:

> *Them:* "*You are **always** late.*"
> *You:* "*No I'm not. I wasn't late **yesterday**.*"

This is an example of context perhaps working against the outcome desired. If the outcome you want is to be corrective and escalate the argument, the "yesterday" quip works. Sure, you can get specific—*or* you can get curious and understand what they actually want from you. You *are* late sometimes. It seems this is upsetting to them. Can you ignore their use of *always* and accept that yes, you have been late more than once and that it causes frustration? Then you can decide what kind of conversation you want to have.

**Broad sweeping statements are common triggers.**

A common practice in conflict is the use of broad sweeping statements like *always, never,* or *you are wrong*—all abstract, vague accusations. Here are some examples of broad sweeping statements that should be avoided because they trigger response rather than clarity:

> *No one around here works hard.*
> *You don't care about profit.*
> *The engineers are hard to work with.*
> *We do not care about our employees.*

**Listen so you *understand* rather than *respond*.**

Sometimes the fastest way to sway an individual during conflict is to stop talking and truly listen. I'm not talking faux listening, which is actually just waiting for a space to say what we think. When we are able to listen to understand with sincere empathy and curiosity, we are investing in future influence. We must have a practice of listening to understand and keep our focus on helping others stay in **listening** mode rather than in **reaction** mode.

Keep people listening longer by avoiding the use of triggering language. We often trigger people into not listening by using vague words that disrupt listening. Here is a common triggering statement:

"Let me play devil's advocate." (Using these buzzwords cause people to get ready to be told they are wrong. Instead, just go right to your idea.)

Instead of:

> Tom, let me play devil's advocate. Won't your idea cause massive attrition?

Try:

> Tom, our attrition is at 13% now. How will a reduction in the free period impact that number?

Or:

> Tom, our attrition is 13%. What safeguards are in your plan to keep that number from sliding?

Do you see how using **context** without triggering a person into feeling **wrong** too soon will keep things conversational a bit longer? Asking Tom for examples instead of telling him he is wrong will keep you ideating rather than fighting.

To keep people listening longer, avoid putting a sentence upfront that triggers them into *not listening*. Here are examples of sentences to avoid:

> Let me play devil's advocate.
> Have you thought of xyz?
> I wouldn't do it that way.
> This isn't a good path for us.
> I disagree with you.

In other words, wait to communicate your point of disagreement. When people feel they are being told they are wrong, they tend to tune out. This is a strategic placement of points within a conversation that can help you keep people's attention long enough to sway them.

**We can use the context rather than the words to listen to the intent of the communication.**

A deliberate practice of using context in conversations means we may be able to move people through conflict faster. If we hear people use broad sweeping statements, we can ask ourselves if perhaps they are right about part of what they are saying. If they are, we can admit rather than defend.

Sometimes it's just faster to admit to something you've done rather than defend it. A specific, heartfelt apology may be in order—and if you persist in being defensive, you may get nowhere.

---

## Here is an example of admission used by listening for context:

---

Them: *You lost all credibility.*
You: *Uh oh, what did I do?*
Them: *You interrupted the CEO.*
You: *Well, the CEO sucks. She keeps interrupting me!*

Really? Is that how this person wants to spend his influence capital—by saying things that make him sound like he's eight years old, sitting in the back seat of a wood-paneled station wagon, fighting with his two older siblings? Sometimes the best context in conflict is, "I did do that. I'm sorry."

Of course, one reason we don't admit when we're wrong is because people use it against us. Another reason we defend rather than admit is because our physiology kicks in and we enter "be right at all costs" mode. Use the Context Model levels to try to get to the example, and if you are wrong in the example, admit it quickly. Example:

Them: *You interrupted the CEO.*

You: *Uh oh. I didn't notice and I don't want to do that. Can you give me more examples so that I can learn?*

## Notice when you are feeling defensive and instead try asking for an example.

Them: *You are not being a good role model for your employees.*

You: *Uh oh. Can you give me an example?*

## Get examples rather than get upset over a broad sweeping statement.

Be curious about what they are **trying** to say rather than upset at what they are **actually** saying. People do not always communicate well when they feel like what they are going to say is difficult. Their physiology may even become weird; then they start using broad sweeping statements to mask real examples that can help you understand what they are really meaning to say.

Remember, in conflict people often say things that are inflammatory or even mean. In order to **use** that moment rather than be abused by it, do not react to everything a person says. If we can get to the specifics of what a person is saying in the midst of conflict, we will likely find something we can **use** to move closer to our desired outcome.

## In conflict, if we can get to the specifics of what they are saying, we will likely find something we can use.

In the above example, imagine if the person responds:

*"I do not have an example; it is just a feeling I have."*

This response makes it really hard to know specifically what to change or think about. The person who told us we were not a good role model doesn't have an example. So now what?

**Without an example, it is hard to know what happens next. If this is the case, use the Context Model to:**

Let her know we want to hear what she is trying to tell us and that without an example, we are stuck. We can ask her to give us an example when she has one.

Or:

We can use the broad sweeping statement as a catalyst for our own learning. Using the Context Model levels, we can convert a vague statement away from a perceived attack and into curiosity.

**Broad sweeping statements can hurt and reduce influence.**

---

Here is an example of how a broad sweeping statement can cause mutual failure in communication:

---

*An employee interrupts his manager during a meeting and tells him that his idea is bull excrement. The manager gets angry—and the problem becomes the employee's profanity rather than the issue at hand. The incompetence the employee was trying to spotlight gets lost in the way he brought it up. Both sides are being irrational: the employee for saying something in a way that creates drama, and the manager for ignoring what the employee was trying to say because he didn't say it right.*

In this example, influence failed. The employee used a broad sweeping statement and didn't talk the way the manager listens; the manager didn't listen to what the employee was trying to say.

Groups and companies are just as guilty of this habit as are individuals.

---

## Here is an example of a mantra that isn't driving new behavior:

---

*ABC Company has an organizational mantra. It isn't on its website, yet if you go out to coffee with leaders in the organization and ask what challenge the company is facing, they all say, "We need to collaborate better."*

The more this statement is passed around, the less the company improves anything. Repetition of this general statement does not lead to an adjustment in behaviors.

## Be careful repeating things to the point that it turns people off.

This habit of repeating things over and over makes a word like *collaboration* into a distant buzzword rather than an action. The more a leader says "collaborate" (or any other buzzword), the less likely people are to change their behavior. These repeated words can then become complaints rather than fixes.

The habit of saying things in a way that fails to get us what we want to be is found in most areas of our lives.

## Here is an example in parenting:

*Often when children have done something adults don't like, adults stand above them and admonish them harshly—and rather than teaching them a lesson, all it does is make them feel the adults' anger.*

*One night Bill asks his son how things went with the babysitter. His son tells him about having a timeout. Bill is interested because he has never used timeouts to motivate his son. He decides to ask a few questions to see what is going on.*

*"What is a timeout, Son?"*

*"It's something adults do when they are having a bad day," his son answers.*

*Bill laughed out loud. His son did not attach the timeout to his own behavior; all he could see was the anger of the sitter. Bill talked with his son about the purpose of a timeout and said, "Let's figure out what behavior caused that to happen since you don't like timeouts. Maybe you can avoid them in the future."*

*His son tells him about throwing peas during lunch. Bill listens and asks a lot of questions. He tells his son a story about the time he and his brother shot peas across the room at each other.*

Why the story? Stories make kids listen. When he had his son in listening mode, his son was more open to hearing other options. We usually use stories to entertain kids, but why not also use storytelling when the message is critical, like with safety and health issues or even when we are angry?

In conflict, using the Context Model will help get to an example and spark curiosity in both parties. When we get the example, we can decide if we agree with the assessment. In the next chapter, we give some additional tips on how to listen when in conflict, so read on.

## A Deliberate Practice

Avoid using broad sweeping statements in your own language. If someone uses a broad sweeping statement with you, become curious: Ask for examples rather than becoming reactive.

## Can I avoid saying broad sweeping statements and get curious when I hear them?

# Chapter Thirteen

# Listen with Context to Improve Outcomes

People often focus on context only when they're talking (as shown in the examples in the previous section). **Listening** with context is important as well—it keeps us curious and brings us closer to understanding the person who's talking to us.

**Levels of context happen in every conversation; start noticing them.**

If you are dealing with someone who lives at a different level of context than you, no problem. Just figure out the pattern and learn to translate; use *her* language, not yours.

---

### Here is an example in pitching an idea:

---

*An investor may want only to hear 'we are optimizing for growth' rather than a lengthy story about how you're doing it.*

**Notice what level of context you are *receiving*.**

Listen for levels of context. If your date says he loves wine, become curious about what kind of wine he likes before trying to impress him with *your* favorite. (Although if you're married, you shouldn't be dating at all. I see that tan line on your finger!)

What the heck was that aside in the above paragraph about? Notice the levels of context that get your attention. Did the "tan line" quip make you more or less interested? Do you listen more when you get specific details, or do you prefer people speaking in general terms?

If a peer says to you, "We have to learn to collaborate better," recognize that you are receiving a high level of context and discuss what actions you can take to improve things instead of just nodding in agreement.

---

## Here is an example of using context to offer a possible solution:

---

*After a meeting one day, Joe says, "We have to learn to collaborate better." You respond, "Agreed! Maybe if we meet three weeks prior to the ship date, we can compare quality concerns and . . ."*

*Listen. Notice.* Help people feel understood and make sure you know what you need to know to move forward.

### Use and ask for examples in your day-to-day life.

Notice if people use superlatives and hyperbole instead of talking about specifics, and when they do, ask them to clarify. Don't be corrective here—just show curiosity.

---

## Here are examples of using curiosity to get specifics:

---

Client: *"We like companies that collaborate with us."*

> You: *"Can you give me an example of a company that collaborated well with you? What did they do?"*
> Or:
> Employee: *"We need to get on this right away."*
> You: *"Why?"* or *"When does it need to be taken care of by?"*
> Or:
> Team member: *"Julie is so patronizing."*
> You: *"How so?"*
> Or:
> Team member: *"It was pure chaos."*
> You: *"What do you mean? Give me an example."*
> *Or simply say, "Tell me."*

Basically, always ask for examples without being totally annoying. (You can reduce your influence if you ask insignificant questions, too. Thus, be mindful that your questions do not feel insignificant or like they are a strategy to make someone feel dumb or attacked.

Examples may also help you when you're in a position of giving or receiving a 'no.' A 'no' with specific examples helps with understanding.

## Be careful forcing people to be specific about insignificant things.

Do not use context as a weapon. If your boss wants to "increase velocity" and uses that phrase frequently, you may not want to ask for specifics to the point that you sound like you're disagreeing. Here is an example of when *not to* ask for specifics:

> Joe is angry. *"Damn it, Carol,"* he says during a one on one, *"we just have to increase velocity!"*

*Instead of agreeing with Joe, Carol, who just fin-*
*ished reading this book, says, "Joe, can you give me*
*a specific example?" Joe's head explodes, and Carol*
*has to clean up all the bits and fragments from the*
*shag carpet in the meeting room. She notices over*
*the next few weeks that Joe isn't really listening to*
*her the way he usually does. Of course! She ticked*
*him off instead of making him feel understood.*

Don't use levels of context if it will cost you influence later. Sometimes people **can't** explain.

## When context is not aligned, we often get triggered in arguments and say stupid things.

If you recognize what your favorite level of context is, you may be less triggered when someone is on an altogether different level of context. For example:

*Carol always got annoyed and immediately dis-*
*engaged from a presentation when anyone used*
*superlatives such as, "We are the **best** at quality of*
*any company on the planet." Carol learned to notice*
*her trigger, however, and when superlatives come*
*up, she now asks questions such as, "What is the*
*percentage of returns on the last three products you*
*created that had more than seven points of distri-*
*bution? Can you describe the most common quality*
*defects you see?" In doing this, Carol drives the con-*
*versation to a level of specifics that works for her and*
*avoids getting annoyed with the person using the*
*superlatives she hates so much.*

## A complaint means a person stands for something.

I love that sentence. A complaint means a person stands for something. I wish I could tell you where I first heard it. I can tell you that sentence has made conflict so much easier for me. I can get curious and get examples when folks are using broad sweeping statements because I search for what they are standing for rather than the perceived jab they are giving me verbally. Here is an example of how a complaint can increase understanding in a relationship:

> Bob says to his wife, "You are parenting all wrong."

> If Angela is able to get curious about what Bob is **standing** for, she will be more likely to get curious about the example instead of defensive and turn the conversation into a confrontation.

> "Uh oh, tell me. How?"
> "You are too controlling. If we do not let him play video games he will just do it behind our back."

> Now Angela is in a conversation that may lead to understanding. Bob is standing for something (his son) although perhaps not saying it in a way that is conducive to good communication.

Humans often communicate things as complaints or accusations when they are upset by something, which can cause us to sound and feel as if we are complaining. These moments can reduce our influence, and theirs. Using the Context Model levels with regard to a complaint can transform a moment of potential annoyance or low leverage into something beautiful. A leader or influencer must excel at turning emotional moments into increased understanding and clarity.

**Use complaints rather than be abused by them.**

When a person is upset and complaining, ask for an example (without sounding like a jerk). Let's imagine that a large company has purchased a small company. Here are three ways of how a complaint can be converted into better outcomes:

Susie, head of product, says, "ABC company doesn't share our values." That little complaint can spread like wildfire and mess with integration.

Ken says, "Susie, tell me what you are seeing." (He is asking for an example in a curious way so that she will elaborate.)

Susie replies, "They gave us a list of approved music we can play at our events. Are you kidding me? Bureaucracy at its worst."

Ken: "Eek. Sounds like litigation at its worst. I imagine that list came from a lawsuit or something. Let's have a conversation about how to be a leader during a transition."

Susie: "We are a company that values **only** sales-people. We treat everyone else like crap."

Ken says, "Tell me, what did you see happen?" Susie gives Ken the example that the company pays $3,000 to any employee who refers a salesperson for a job, yet only $300 for all other positions.

## Use complaints to increase influence.

People have a basic need to feel understood. Letting them talk more and asking them to give specifics increases their feeling of being understood. If we give them that feeling, it can increase our influence.

If people are truly upset, sometimes they will move through their discomfort more quickly if they focus on an example. The Context Model levels tell us to ask for examples—good practice for any influencer.

It doesn't make sense to blindly accept a broad sweeping complaint at face value. Doing so can often end a conversation, which can lead to the complainer feeling misunderstood. If you get an example, you're more likely to be able to address the real issue.

---

### Here is an example of using levels of context to drive behavior:

---

Example without using Levels of Context:

Son: *I hate school.*
Mom: *You have to go. School is good for you.*
*Son walks away, goes to his room, and soothes himself by playing* Minecraft.

Example using Levels of Context:

Son: *I hate school.*
Mom: *Tell me, honey, what part?*
Son: *Well, today a substitute teacher got mad at us for being loud. She yelled at us to be quiet and I was quiet. Then she made us all put our hands over our mouths. I wouldn't do it. Then she came over and screamed at me to put my hand over my mouth. I told her I was doing what she asked, being quiet, and that I didn't feel comfortable putting my hand over my mouth. She sent me to the principal's office.*

Mom: *Yikes. That sounds like an adult out of control. I'd hate school too if I had been through that. How about we go chat with the principal tomorrow? Let's make sure he sees this situation the way we do.*

*Or:*
*Son: I hate school.*
*Mom: Tell me, honey, what part?*
*Son: The kids are really mean to me; they won't let me play with them during kickball.*
*Mom: Ouch. Yuck. Tell me more.*

A complaint means a person stands for something: Find out what that is. **Listen for complaints and ask for specifics.**

## To increase influence, be careful of sounding like you are complaining.

So far, I have been talking about listening for a complaint and getting examples to understand what the person is saying. Be careful of sounding like *you* are complaining, though, because not everyone can see what you are standing for when you are complaining and may not listen well to complaints.

## Understand the difference between feedback and complaint.

---

**Here is an example of an earnest request sounding like a complaint:**

---

*We do not collaborate well.*

This is a complaint. Although people may agree with it, nothing really changes after we say it. Instead, use the Context Model levels to increase action.

---

### Here is an example of how to make a request that doesn't sound like a complaint:

---

*Let's meet every Friday to discuss the deliberate tradeoffs we are making to hit the deadline: you and I and the head of product get in a room and hash it out.*

That is more specific and action-focused. Avoid sounding as if you are complaining; instead, use specifics to incite action.

## A Deliberate Practice

Focus on what people are standing for when they are complaining. Ask for examples and get them to talk more.

## Can I get curious about a complaint and use context to get to an example?

# Chapter Fourteen

# Levels of Context Practice for Parents

The fastest way to lose an audience is to tell them how to parent. NOTHING in this list is to tell you how to parent. I am not a parental expert and thus I offer zero parenting advice. You know your kid and what you are doing is right.

Below are some ideas to play with that may not be the right ones for your kid. Yet, to get really great at something in business, it helps if we practice it all the time. If you have little ones at home, practicing Levels of Context in interactions with them will help you develop more of a habit when needing to use it at work.

**A quick list of ways to practice the Levels of Context model in parenting:**

### Storytelling

A.   Opinion Last Storytelling: Kids seem to listen intently during story time. Practice teaching kids using storytelling that isn't too obvious about the moral of the story. Tell the story with relish and then if there is a moral, say it in one sentence, at the end. See if you can get the kids so focused on the story that they learn without being specifically told what they are supposed to learn.

B.    Teach your kids how to storytell: Storytelling is a required business skill these days. Teach your kids how to create stories and relive them. Teach them the Context Model. It could even help them in dating (ha) and in writing class.

C.    Storytelling at dinner time: Have each person at the dinner table tell one story from their day. This can be a hilarious habit that gives a parent information, connection and practices storytelling.

D.    Ask questions that get examples: Instead of "how was your day?" ask something like "what happened today that made you laugh so hard you snorted?" Create a list of the types of questions that your kid responds to.

### Encouraging behaviors

E.    Spotlight the behavior you want to see: Be highly verbal and consistent about the specific, deliberate activity that you want to see.

     Example: *When I have 5 boys over for a play date, I make a BIG DEAL when they are generous and helpful to one another. I will pull one of them aside randomly and make a huge deal if they give a toy, help another kid, etc. Over time, the kids want the kudos so they do more generous actions.*

F.  Give feedback with specific examples: Avoid labels, superlative-only and character comments. Give specific examples of what they are doing well or can adjust. (See feedback section for more on this.)

G.  Use the rewind button: Have them reverse storytell a situation.

Example: *"Jimmy, I noticed that you got in more trouble for hitting your sister than she did for taking your toy. Let's rewind and tell the story another way. What can you rewrite here? How can you do this differently?*

Use the principles of storytelling to help them love this process. Kids are hilarious when they story tell with reckless abandon. My son once rewound a story and in that story the dust mites under the refrigerator rose up to fight the tyranny of bed time.

## Empathy

H.  Use context to express empathy: The next time your kid is upset about something, use context to express empathy and acknowledge the feeling.

*Example: Johnny is upset that the peas are touching the carrots. Instead of telling him to eat them anyway, practice playing with empathy to see if Johnny can move through the temporary upset. "Johnny, you do not like for your food to mix and it is upsetting. I'm so sorry honey." Often, kids will reduce their upset when we acknowledge the feeling. Then we can coach them. "Tell me more about the*

*peas and the carrots honey. Tell me the story . . ."*
*Kids will often tell hilarious reasons why they are*
*upset. We fill their basic need to feel understood and*
*sometimes they will move to ideas on how to solve it*
*after they express their upset.*

We'd love to hear the stories your kids come up with. If you
want to share, email us. Our contact info is at the end of this
book.

## A Deliberate Practice

Get curious about giving or getting examples
when interacting with children.

# How can I use
# Levels of Context in parenting?

# Chapter Fifteen

# Summary of Habits to Do and Not Do

A quick summary of the Context Model level habits to look for:

**Influence-reducing habits to watch out for:**
- Buzzwords
- Complaints
- Broad, sweeping statements
- Superlatives
- Talking *about it* vs. being *in it*
- Generalizations
- All or nothings
- Patronization and condescension
- Making people feel small or insignificant
- Pandering or being political

**Habits that increase listening:**
- Examples
- Experiential storytelling: *reliving it* vs. *reciting* it
- Curiosity (getting the other person talking)
- Asking vs. telling

- Using the other person's buzzwords
- Asking for examples when someone uses a buzzword
- Being vivid—using phrases that stick
- Specific, detailed
- Understand **and** repeat
- Helping people find themselves in what we are saying
- Visuals
- Being open and curious about the other person

## *How will I remember to use Levels of Context in my day-to-day influence?*

# Chapter Sixteen

# What Now?

Now that you have read this book, here are some suggestions about how you can use it:

- From this moment forward, consider each communication moment as a chance to sway—an interaction between people meant to move toward a better outcome.
- Notice if communication is not going the way you want and ask yourself if the Context Model levels could help you increase understanding and influence.
- When using one of the skills described here to gain influence such as presentations or conflict, re-read the section that discusses that skill.
- Select one deliberate practice and focus on it until it becomes a habit.

## How does Levels of Context show up in the conversation I'm having?

### Summary of Deliberate Practice questions for each chapter.

- Chapter One: What is the *outcome* and how do I use what is happening to move closer to the outcome?
- Chapter Two: Am I *open* or closed?

- Chapter Three: What makes the person I want to influence listen more? What makes them check out?
- Chapter Four: Am I investing in this person's basic need to feel understood by listening more?
- Chapter Five: Am I being specific?
- Chapter Six: Can I look for the opposite of any label I have so I see more of reality?
- Chapter Seven: What is one influence-reducing habit I can reduce?
- Chapter Eight: Can I notice Levels of Context in conversations and conflict and push for understanding?
- Chapter Nine: Can I keep a journal of examples and stories with lots of specific details I find interesting to use in future presentations?
- Chapter Ten: Can I practice asking questions or giving feedback with specific actionable examples?
- Chapter Eleven: How specific are my instructions, and is it clear who is specifically accountable?
- Chapter Twelve: Can I avoid saying broad sweeping statements and get curious when I hear them?
- Chapter Thirteen: Can I get curious about a complaint and use context to get to an example?
- Chapter Fourteen: How can I use Levels of Context in parenting?
- Chapter Fifteen: How will I remember to think Levels of Context in my day-to-day influence?
- Chapter Sixteen: How does Levels of Context show up in the conversation I am having?

**Below is an empty Levels of Context model for you to use as you practice using Levels of Context.**

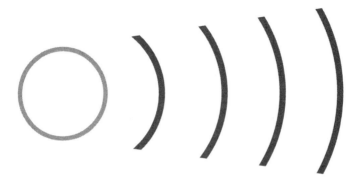

*Levels of Context poster available at allegoryinc.com*

# About the Author

Christina Harbridge is the founder of Allegory, Inc., a behavior change company. We are a gaggle of humans who understand that humans are beautifully irrational and emotional, and we recognize that when we are triggered, we do things that move us away from the outcome we want. Allegory, Inc. creates tools to harness this natural emotion and physiology and use it to increase influence and leadership, bringing us *closer* to the outcome we want. Our deliberate practice as a team is to stay curious to the learning in every situation. Our intellectual property came from the various life experiences described below.

*There are no commas after my name.*

I am a hack. There are no commas after my name. Nothing I say can be considered professional advice. My only real credential is an incessant curiosity and desire to keep myself safe and in control by creating an if/then statement for human behavior.

A few things from my history inform my belief systems about influence.

*I was in speech therapy as a child.*

It wasn't a lot of fun leaving my class every day to go to special education. I was teased, especially by two kids named

Hope and Gus. The more focus the speech therapist put on my stammer, the worse it became. One day in the car with my Aunt Rosie on my way to be a daffodil in the school play, I was sick with worry. (I don't know who thought it was a good idea to put a kid with a stammer onstage.) As I sat on the floor in that back seat of the car, I noticed Aunt Rosie's boots—leather cutouts revealed a turquoise color beneath. I was so transfixed by the specific patterns that I noticed I was no longer sick to my stomach. Looking at the detail of something eased my nerves.

I began to practice getting out of my head as a means to address my nerves. One day I lived in my head in generalities, and the next I lived outside my head in a realm of specifics. This tiny deliberate practice of watching the detail of what I liked around me fixed my stammer and fed me so much data about how people listen. Now I see a lot of detail. I notice how people react in communication and conflict, and I have compiled decades of notes on it. I have taken all this noticing and categorized it into a nonscientific way of interpreting how physiology is connected to our linguistics. We call this Somatic Linguistics, and it is an art, not a science.

*My dad believed in infiltrating rather than in protesting.*

My dad was a civil rights activist. He would beat people up for racial discrimination at a public pool. Then one day he realized that no one changes by way of force. He couldn't do the nonviolent thing, yet he also felt that *forcing* people to change caused them to do so unwillingly and slowly. So, one day he joined the very group he wanted to change—he created intimacy between himself and those he disagreed with. In small moments of reducing anonymity between them, he found he held influence and could change the rules from the inside. I watched him deal efficiently with conflict in a way that removed the *us* and *them*. I am proud of him for that.

*I started a collection agency that collected debt by being nice.*
My dad had Parkinson's disease and his health was failing. I got scared. I looked around at his local nursing homes, and the ones we could afford on his retirement were simply unacceptable—eighteen people to a room, with only sheets separating their beds. Unable to stand the thought of my dad in such a demeaning place, I shifted to being a night student and set out to make some real money. I answered an ad at a collection agency. Although the people I met were nice, they were awful once they got on the phone to make collections. Their negativity really bothered me. I got it in my head that with so many calls going out in the world, this company should be doing its part to spread positivity. After a failed attempt with a business partner (long story there), I ultimately decided to start my own collection agency with a strong human relations philosophy. We helped people find jobs, listened to them, tried to help them, and sometimes got invited to their weddings. We worked from the premise that humans have a basic need to feel understood and if we stopped focusing on collecting money, genuine empathy and a listening ear would turn an angry caller into a payment. We focused on establishing enough of a relationship with the people so they would tell us the truth, and from that place of honesty we could have a productive conversation about their next steps. When we gave bonuses to people based on the number of thank-you cards they received instead of money they collected, we actually increased the money collected. It dawned on me how truly inauthentic and backward most

communication patterns were and as such, how little influence and productivity resulted from them.

*Helping artists and doing art helped me realize that influence requires a reduction in us and them.*
I learned I could hang off a 31-foot art sculpture and weld metal into shapes. That felt easy compared to convincing a city employee behind the counter to give us a permit. Such began a period of helping a group of artists get their work to the world, and it was my dad's theory of infiltration that came to the rescue when that battle got tough. By *joining* the folks behind the bureaucratic counter and making them feel like *a part* of the creativity and beauty, permit processes for the art installations went much more smoothly. While dealing with incredible artists on the one hand and suits on the other, I realized how often the *us and them* mentality makes it hard to influence people who aren't like us. If we truly hear people's stories, we'll realize they're more like us than they are different. I learned that we are always just one story away from our closest friends and tucked that lesson away in my arsenal of communication theory.

*A big part of influence and leadership is dictated by our physiology and emotion.*
When I was (very lucky to be) a NASA test subject, I got to wear a cool jacket that tests 22 elements of human physiology and anatomy. I geeked out over everything I didn't know about our bodies. Thankfully, the nice folks at NASA let me mess around with the equipment while waiting to do zero gravity. In my collection agency, I used Heartmath technology to test some of my silly theories on the physical responses to conflict when on the job. Playing in this sandbox and learning about

my bodily responses to different situations convinced me that we can *use* our emotions rather than be abused by them. I believe our physiology beautifully activates to teach us stuff, yet most of us have been taught to numb that data. Each activation is *for* us, not *to* us. When we get curious about how we feel, we are less reactive and thereby more able to influence.

*People started hiring me.*

One day an elected official hired me to teach his team communication after he watched me "woo" them in a meeting. So, I started teaching folks exactly what we had been doing at my agency that turned a collection call into a wedding invitation. I began to get more of these requests, and then more after that.

Folks hired me to help them get elected; to do TED talks; and to train people in conflict, leadership learning, and more. Sometimes I had no idea what I was doing. Sometimes I was fired when my good ideas trumped how my coachees felt about themselves. But I learned with every engagement. I learned *a lot*.

For more than a decade I ran my collection agency and taught people how to communicate based on the stuff I learned there. Then, everything changed when my son was born. As CEO of a growing agency, I had woken up each day excited and terrified to go to work even though I thrived on it, but as a mother I could no longer carry a large payroll and decided I had too much going on to be CEO material. So, I sold the company and kept all my intellectual property about influence/conflict, etc.

*How people feel about themselves dictates a lot of influence.*

Being a mom has solidified my belief that the way people listen is inextricably linked with how they feel about themselves around the person who is talking. For example, so many of my impulses around parenting are simply an imitation of what I'd experienced from my own parents. I realized that my reactions as a parent were actually teaching my son to comply and to *not* talk to me. I believe one of my primary responsibilities as a parent is to establish an environment in which my son feels comfortable telling me anything. Yet, my impulse was often to numb the tough conversations. Why?

*I was raised in the "just get over it" generation.*

I was raised simply to be happy. For my parents—and society at the time—happiness was paramount, even at the cost of authenticity. As a child, it felt as though any person experiencing an emotion not palatable to others would be disregarded or shut down altogether. This seems so irrational to me. Emotions exist. They are what they are and can't be what they are not. So why not work *with* them?

Beauty is often on the other side of an emotion if we sit in it for a few seconds. Still, I watch company cultures falter because of their inability to acknowledge real emotions and therefore their inability to function in reality. How can there be productivity without first facing the reality of a situation? It's the job of company representatives to know when their employees are being driven by emotion and to have the tools to move through those cases rather than avoid them. I have the same job as a parent: to know when my son's emotions are making him irrational, to accept those emotions as an opportunity for growth, to navigate them rather than sweeping them under the rug, and to confront reality by allowing emotion to exist in the moment. It is my job as a parent to teach my son to know when he is irrational and emotional and to know how to move through it rather than soothe or go around it. Contrary to what my parents taught me, drinking a lot of Long Island Iced Tea will not turn unwanted emotions into happiness. I want my son to know that.

"Just be happy" and "just get over it" leave people unable to *feel* the nuances of their physiology that tell them they are about to be reactive. We need a better strategy.

*I have avoided grief most of my life; I am imperfect.*

In order to fully live and love, I must learn three crucial lessons: grief, empathy and forgiveness.

Like any family, mine had its share of loss. When my brother Sean died from a gunshot in our home, everything that was already broken fell apart completely. When my dad became disabled with Parkinson's, I thought about his impending death every day. When my brother Gary died on a motorcycle, I blamed myself for not insisting he wear a helmet. When a family member was facing an impossible situation, I refused to acknowledge how difficult it was for her by being relentlessly positive. I am still sorry for that to this day. To some degree I've taken responsibility for every loss in my life as a way to avoid the devastation of grief. Just being sad without the ability to fix anything didn't suit my inner control freak.

I have been petty. I've shunned people I love out of fear. I've shunned people who love me because of my inability to deal with emotions. I struggle with being an expert in conflict to my clients because often I fail at it in my own home and personal life, and there was a time when I used a glass of wine to drown my conflicts, although I didn't address them at all. (A glass of wine as a treat is a beautiful thing for me; a glass of wine to numb emotions messes with my genius.)

I've mishandled relationships and failed to communicate

when I was not happy. I lost people close to me because I was unable to ask for what I needed. I often knew how to set boundaries only with anger and avoidance. The ability to sit in acceptance of these facts and still believe in myself is a daily practice. I'm a badass who knows how to turn a challenging moment into something awesome (and is sharing that gift with the world), yet what I most need to learn is that I am lovable for who I am, not for what I do.

*So, basically I'm an afraid six-year-old girl in a woman's body.*

I'm afraid that I'm a fraud. I'm afraid that I'll be found out and attacked. I'm afraid that two years from now, I'll look at the body of work I created and find it terribly stupid. But at the same time, I am unafraid. I can be pompous and arrogant, too—certain that my ways are the right ways. Both of these identities live in one aging body I've got to call home. I firmly believe most of us can improve our emotional literacy, including me.

So, dear reader, here is my request: Be skeptical. Don't believe everything I say. The stuff on these pages isn't tested by experts. Just try it and see if it helps increase your influence even 5% of the time. If it does, maybe it was worth the read.

Thank you for reading this book. I do not want our relationship to end here on this cold, sterile page.

I LOVE to hear from people. Your stories, examples and questions. Follow and communicate with us on Twitter @charbridge @allegoryinc or on Facebook @allegoryinc #swayed.

I will respond to questions, although without my rock star editor, the responses may be grammatically challenged.

# Acknowledgments

Appreciation and acknowledgment are the foundation of my values as a human. If I were to write an acknowledgment of all of the humans who have touched my heart and given me encouragement to write this book, we'd need ten volumes. On this page are the people whom, without them, this book would not have happened. I am not a good enough writer to ever properly express my gratitude to these beautiful humans:

- First and foremost, whatever I did to be in Christine Bronstein's orbit, it was not enough. Thank you, Christine, for believing not just in me, but in countless other women you have helped, you are magic.
- If the editor Mickey Nelson would have written this acknowledgment, it would likely make you tear up or something. She has such talent in editing my drivel into this book.
- If you look up the word integrity in the dictionary, you will see a picture of Sonia Swanson. For almost a decade she has helped me find my True North with her incessant questions and solid value system.
- Pat and Michelle Cooley, two people who inspire me to be more spiritual, read the book before it was done and gave me such specific and actionable encouragement.
- As a child I watched my dad's best friend Tchaka Muhammed stand in the middle of a crowded room and

(without amplification) begin to whisper a story. He'd have the entire room mesmerized as he helped us feel our way into a tale. So much of my beliefs about storytelling are from watching a master.

- My dad tacked Rudyard Kipling's poem *If*—to my wall and referred to it often when life got tricky. I can see that poem, and my dad's love, in between the lines in this book. Dad, you taught me the power of love and infiltration. I love you more, etc. I win.
- My son told me when he was a toddler, "Momma, when you are sad and act like you are happy, I know you are sad." Sebastian James Law, you have taught me more about emotional literacy and being a human who sees feelings as delicious than anything else in my life. I am so proud to be your Mom. ILYMEP. (And I will get you back on the bottle of water prank, just you wait.)